SACRED SOIL

To my parents
Reg and Joyce Finlay

SACRED SOIL
Images and Stories of the
New Zealand Wars

Neil Finlay

RANDOM
HOUSE
NEW ZEALAND LTD

Special thanks to:
Al and Bev Young, Rhondda Bosworth, Mark Adams, my brother and sister John and Kaye Finlay,
Bill Gruar, Elizabeth McKlintock, Angus Blair-Butler, Robert Laing and family, Dan Panapa, Jim and
Ngaio Tairawhiti, Leone Blair, the staff of the Tarankai, Hawkes Bay, Te Awamutu and Auckland
Museums, the staff of the Alexander Turnbull Library, members of the Irish band 'Feck',
and very special thanks to my partner Crissi.

A RANDOM HOUSE BOOK
Published by
Random House New Zealand
18 Poland Road, Glenfield, Auckland, New Zealand

First published 1998

ISBN 1 86941 357 1

Printed in Hong Kong

The author welcomes correspondence arising from this book: picker@ihug.co.nz

Contents

Preface

Most of my working life I've been a musician, and I've spent a lot of that time going up and down New Zealand in various rock, country and blues bands. Although the pay was usually lousy, exploring a country such as this with guitar in hand was a valuable experience. I met many wonderful people and visited places that were well off the tourist track. New Zealand is great for this kind of adventure. It's big enough to give you freedom to move, and small enough to get to know it well. In spite of this there are still many places I haven't seen — there are very few gigs north of Dargaville, and I've yet to be offered one at Milford Sound.

As I graduated from being a young rock and roller to an ageing one, I started to take a bit of an interest in this country I call home. Travelling through areas like the West Coast of the South Island, or the Mackenzie Country or the King Country, I wondered what these places were like 100 years ago. History at secondary school was pretty watered-down stuff, and I can remember thinking then that it was full of imperial arrogance.

So I started reading New Zealand history books, such as James Cowan's *The New Zealand Wars and the Pioneering Period* and James Belich's *The New Zealand Wars and the Victorian Interpretation of Racial Conflict*. This latter book had a profound effect on how I see this country. Now I had a new hobby — collecting and reading history books.

Another hobby was photography. This remained latent for a long time, until I saw work by brilliant New Zealand photographers such as Peter Black, Robin Morrison and, more recently, Mark Adams. These people had photographed many of the places I had visited, and when I saw their photos, my own interest in photography started to grow way out of proportion to my ability. In an effort to improve, I took myself off for a couple of years to study the subject. It is that study which has led to this book.

There is nothing in the text of this book that is new — to say something new was not my intention. Rather my starting point offers a fresh angle: for this book is a result of re-exploring this country from a historical point of view. This time I left the guitar at home and instead took a couple of cameras.

When the first Europeans arrived here they saw that it was to their advantage to respect the culture of their hosts. The first traders and missionaries who set up shop on these shores were absorbed into the Maori communities, and with the flow of trade that followed, it was a deal that worked well for Pakeha and Maori alike. Eventually more and more people arrived and settled here, and as their numbers grew, so did the need for land. Respect for the owners of the land started to wane, and eventually war broke out.

This book is about that war. It's also a travelogue — a tour of most of the important battle sites around the country. It's not trying to be definitive but a good sampling of the wars and the traces they have left on our physical and social landscape. The history of New Zealand is rich and exciting. It is also tragic, and needs to be confronted.

These days, of course, there are still many areas in New Zealand where the ownership of the land is under dispute. We are involved in a process to settle these disputes, a process that is too slow for some and perhaps too quick for others. Maybe if we have a better understanding of our past, it will help us to see where we are going today.

The New Zealand Wars happened not that long ago, in terms of history, and I hope this book serves as a reminder that the signs of our turbulent past are still very much with us.

Many of the sites I visited, in particular the battle sites, are places sacred to the Maori, and where possible I made sure that I had permission from them before I traipsed all over the place taking photos. At times I could find no one to speak to, so I relied on my own intuition — and indeed there are places that I did not photograph because it 'didn't feel right'. If you are visiting these places, please respect them. The atmosphere that exists at many of them will tell you that you are on sacred soil.

Northland

When I was a kid I fell through the wharf at Russell. Not all the way through — I got stuck halfway and the little black barnacles that surrounded the hole I went through cut one of my legs to ribbons as I went down, and repeated the process as I was pulled back up. It was very painful, but the pain wasn't as bad as the total embarrassment of it all. This incident is still occasionally remembered at family gatherings, and is still a source of amusement for them. Of course the wharf is in much better shape now, catering as it does to the thousands of tourists who flock to this paradise each year.

It was November when I visited this beautiful place to take the photos that appear here. The settlement of Russell was bracing itself for the summer tourist season: in-season prices had kicked in, and there was a 'calm before the storm' atmosphere about the place.

The first place I went to was the flagstaff on Maiki Hill, which was swarming with busloads of school children accompanied by harassed teachers, and a few early tourists. As the school kids left to go down to the beach, I heard one of the teachers say, 'Stay off the wharf until we all get there.' It sounded like good advice to me.

I stayed and watched the sun go down and thought about how, a hundred or so years ago, the harbour would have been teeming with fish and the surrounding ground fit to grow anything. Ever since there have been people here, there has been fighting over this area. I found it hard to blame them.

During the first four decades of the nineteenth century the European population of New Zealand was sparse. It consisted mainly of traders and missionaries, and these people were welcome, and indeed highly valued, as members of the communities in which they settled. Any Maori tribe or tribal group which had a trader or a missionary living in its midst had access to trade goods, so it was in their interests to make sure that he remained happy and healthy — unless, of course, he got out of line. The traders themselves realised that they lived under the sufferance of the Maori, and the wise ones were careful not to break or interfere with any tribal customs. In short, they tended to adopt the Maori lifestyle and become Pakeha–Maori.

The balance of power was soon to change, however. Initially few Maori converted to Christianity, but gradually the numbers grew. Some openly embraced the new religion, and many saw studying with the missionaries as a way of learning more about European society. During their stay in this country the missionaries had ample opportunity to acquire vast land holdings, and many lost no time in doing so.

While the missionaries were importing the first Bibles into Aotearoa, other traders brought many other items, including the musket. Muskets had a huge impact on Maori society: they became a necessity, since those who had them held a distinct advantage over those who didn't. This eventually caused a power imbalance that led to the Musket Wars — in 1818 tribal tension erupted into warfare that lasted well into the 1830s, and ended only when all the tribes involved had access to the guns.

Flax was used to buy guns — a ton of dressed flax equalled one musket. As the survival of a tribe depended on owning guns, flax production absorbed most of the labour that would normally be used for other purposes, such as growing food.

European 'civilisation' had arrived.

Traders and missionaries were not the only Europeans to find themselves on these shores. Escaped convicts and sailors who jumped ship were also integrated into Maori society, but their situation was somewhat different. If a Pakeha was found to have little or no value as a trader, they became slaves, and generally speaking had a hard time of it. They were sometimes sold back to traders.

One such trader was Hans Tapsell, who had set up a successful business at Maketu. The going rate for a Pakeha was around twenty pounds, and Hans Tapsell would give many of these newly acquired and grateful Pakeha work within his own operation. Not all turned out to be a good bargain.

THE TREATY OF WAITANGI

On 6 February 1840 the first signatures were collected for the Treaty of Waitangi and the process of annexation of Aotearoa by the British Government had begun. The Treaty was presented as two versions: one in the Maori language and one in English. With the translation of the two versions, discrepancies emerge. Amongst other disputed differences, the Maori version states that, although New Zealand now came under the sovereignty of Britain, the Maori were to retain authority over the land. In the English version, however, sovereignty and authority were in effect transferred to Queen Victoria.

Tiriti o Waitangi Marae.

For the time being at least, things remained as they were. Governor FitzRoy did not have the resources or the inclination to enforce British law on the Maori. Within a few years, though, a series of events was to increase tension between Maori and the New Zealand colonial government. The capital, centred in the Bay of Islands, was moved to Auckland and many traders diverted business to the new centre. This coincided with a downturn in trade with Australia, and affected the economy of Northland.

The colonial government introduced customs duties which were to be collected from foreign vessels. This was money that was once collected by the Ngapuhi. A tax on land sales was also introduced, in a move that was unpopular with Maori and settlers alike. Laws had been passed which banned the sale of land except through the government — a move that enraged the Ngapuhi, who saw it for what it was: direct interference. FitzRoy lacked the resources to enforce such laws, and allowed private land sales to continue, but these sales were initially taxed at ten shillings per acre. This duty was reduced to a penny per acre in the face of massive opposition, but the damage had been done. Further interference took the form of restrictions on the felling of timber.

Many Maori felt it was all becoming a bit much. One of those who was discontented was Hone Heke — and he had little trouble finding support.

The flagstaff on Maiki Hill.

HONE HEKE AND KAWITI

Hone Heke was educated at the Waimate mission. He was literate and, as a Christian convert, he knew the Bible well. He had plans to buy a schooner and set up a trading business, but due to the downturn in trade throughout the area, he was unable to do so. He and many others were unhappy with the amount of British interference they were being subjected to.

When British authorities arrested, tried and hanged a Maori chief for the murder of a woman by the name of Robinson and her two children, as well as a young Maori boy, it was felt that the matter should have been handled by the Maori themselves. The young Maori who was murdered was the grandson of another chief called Rewa, a great warrior, and it was up to the Maori to exact utu. The man chosen to avenge this insult was Heke.

To complicate matters further, one of Heke's slaves, a woman, had gone to live with a settler in Kororareka (now Russell). Heke went there with a war party to reclaim her, or at least to be compensated. Some pigs were stolen and a war dance was performed during which some of the white women of the community witnessed the exposure of private parts. Though not forced to watch the dance they were none the less very offended.

The following day, 8 July 1844, Hone Heke cut down the flagstaff for the first time.

Hone Heke was the one who originally provided the flagstaff on Maiki Hill. Its initial purpose was to fly the flag of the United Tribes. The fact that the flagstaff, which stood on Maori ground, now flew the Union Jack was considered a grave insult by Heke.

Heke's war was not with the settlers of the region, however — it was with the British Government. This was the main reason that the flagstaff was cut down — as a symbol of Heke's frustration. Throughout the northern war Hone Heke did what he could to protect the white settlers of the region. Kawiti, Heke's ally in this war, however, was not as generous. If Heke was the inspiration for the Northern war, then Kawiti was the military genius behind it.

Kawiti was of the old school. He was not a Christian convert and had little time for the settlers and the 'civilisation' they brought with them. In reference to the British army he stated that he would not be happy until he had killed a hundred of them. As will be seen, it was this man who was to develop strategies and methods of fighting the British that would be used in the wars throughout New Zealand. After the battle at Ruapekapeka, a model was made of the Ruapekapeka Pa and sent to other areas of the country, allowing other tribes to pick up Kawiti's technology and apply it to their own fighting pa.

The flagstaff was re-erected, this time by British troops, and Heke felt duty bound to cut it down again. He did so in January 1845. The cutting down of the flagstaff caused great alarm, and Governor FitzRoy started moving what troops he could into the area. FitzRoy also had the support of another section of the Ngapuhi, under the control of Tamati Waka Nene.

Like Heke, Waka Nene wanted to protect the interests of the white settlers of Northland, though his support for FitzRoy probably stemmed more from a hatred of Heke than from a love for the British. Hone Heke and Waka Nene had had their differences in the past and the dispute between them was on a personal level. When the flagstaff was erected once more it was Waka Nene's troops who protected it, though they stood aside when it was felled for the third time just prior to the attack on Kororareka.

On 11 March 1845 at 4 am the anti-government forces of Heke and Kawiti attacked Kororareka. The attacking force was in three groups, the first of which, under Kawiti, surprised the naval detachment from the HMS *Hazard* guarding the southern entrance to the settlement. The sailors and marines under Commander Robertson were forced from their position, but fought their way back. Robertson was badly wounded and eventually they had to retire.

The soldiers from the blockhouse at the foot of Maiki Hill had come out to see what was going on, and when they returned to the blockhouse they found it occupied by a second group of Maori, who were firing on another blockhouse nearby that was manned by civilians and old soldiers.

In the meantime the third group in the attacking force, under Heke, had gathered on the top of Maiki Hill, and the flagstaff was again felled. All three groups then took cover, and fire was exchanged for several hours until the ammunition supply at one of the blockhouses was accidentally blown up. One of the soldiers in the blockhouse was smoking while handling the gunpowder supply. A spark dropped from his pipe onto the floor, which was spattered with spilt powder from the kegs; the powder ignited, and up it went.

With Commander Robertson wounded, Lieutenant Philpotts took charge and the soldiers and inhabitants of the town were evacuated to the *Hazard* and other ships which were in the bay at the time. The evacuation itself went smoothly, and there are reports that some of the Maori, including Heke himself, helped civilians to the ships offshore. Once on board the *Hazard*, Philpotts ordered a bombardment of the town, setting it alight, while onshore the victorious Maori were engaged in plundering the stores of food and rum that had been left behind. The following morning the ships set sail for Auckland.

With the sacking of Kororareka, the fledgling colony had lost its fifth-largest town, and 50,000 pounds' worth of property had been destroyed. It was a huge blow. Lieutenant Philpotts, whose eccentric character emerges from this history, came under criticism for

Kororareka in 1836. Making New Zealand Collection, Alexander Turnbull Library F320-1/2-MNZ.

The oldest church in New Zealand at Kororareka, still bearing bullet holes from the attack, and surrounded by graves of those who died in the fighting.

Sketch of the action at Puketutu. Alexander Turnbull Library F-95465-1/2.

Puketutu battlefield today.

the evacuation of the town, which was considered premature, as well as for the bombardment, which was considered unnecessary. Ensign Campbell, who commanded the garrison at the blockhouse, also came under severe criticism for leaving his post. It would appear that with British military defeats, hindsight is 20/20. It would also appear that following British defeats — and there were to be a few — officers, soldiers, and government officials would all blame each other, without acknowledging that they were up against a foe that had simply out-fought and out-thought them.

PUKETUTU

After the cutting down of the flagstaff at Kororareka, FitzRoy had decided that Heke must be punished, and had sent for reinforcements: 215 men of the 58th Regiment had arrived on 22 April 1845. With the sacking of Kororareka, however, FitzRoy was now determined to stop Heke once and for all.

The British army sailed for the Bay of Islands. Three hundred regular soldiers, 40 European volunteers and 120 seamen and marines landed there on 3 May and started off to Heke's pa at Puketutu on the shore of Lake Omapere, 15 miles away. Because of foul weather and the condition of the track, it took four days for them to arrive at Puketutu and join up with Waka Nene's forces.

Finding the site at Puketutu today is not easy. There are no obvious markers or signs. I drove up and down the stretch of road by the lake several times, and there was a fair bit of head-scratching going on. Eventually I put my ego aside and asked one or two people for directions, but they were unable to help. They looked at me with that expression that said they knew I was from Auckland. I had with me James Cowan's two volumes of The New Zealand Wars *and in them I found a sketch of the battle that also gave clues to where the site was. I chose what looked a likely spot and photographed it, hoping that I was right. Subsequent research confirmed that I was at least very close. The site is on private land about 4 kilometres south of Okaihau, where the road is as close as it gets to Lake Omapere.*

Tamati Waka Nene and his followers had built a pa on Heke's land at the spot where the Okaihau township now sits, and he had started his own campaign against Heke's forces. The fighting between Waka Nene and Heke was more in the nature of a feud than open warfare. Prisoners were returned and there were no ambushes or fighting after dark. When the British army under the command of Lieutenant-Colonel Hulme arrived on the scene, all that was about to change.

Waka Nene watched with interest as the imperial army prepared for battle. He wasn't overly impressed with what he saw. For a start, the soldiers were standing around while they were eating. Before Maori went into battle, the meal would be eaten sitting down, as if it were just another day. And when he saw troops moving into position for the attack, he noticed that some of them carried stretchers. This was just asking for trouble. At the battle of Puketutu, Waka Nene chose not to get involved and instead watched from the sidelines.

Hulme set some of his force on a low ridge facing the pa, and firing started. There was no artillery to force a breach in the palisade surrounding the pa, but some rockets were fired at it, without success. Heke watched with apparent amusement as the rockets, a fairly new weapon in the British armoury, shot off uncontrolled in all directions. One of them eventually found its way into the pa and was the cause of much smoke and confusion, but no damage.

The earlier fighting with Waka Nene meant that Heke had been unable to complete construction of the pa, and it was thought that the side facing the lake was the weak point. Hulme decided to launch an assault there, and 216 selected men were sent around the pa to attack. The assault group made their way via the swampy ground on the lake shore — a difficult manœuvre — and were about to launch the attack when Kawiti attacked from the rear.

Kawiti had arrived at Puketutu the day before the British and had elected to camp in the bush behind the pa, not in the pa itself. The attack from the rear took the British by surprise. They turned, and with a series of volleys followed by fighting at close quarters, managed to force Kawiti's men back to the bush. Heke sent some of his force from the pa as a counterattack and the British had to turn again to fight them off. Meantime Kawiti regrouped and attacked again. The British army were good at this type of fighting — they had had plenty of practice in the wars of Europe — and fought off each of these attacks, inflicting heavy casualties among Kawiti's and Heke's followers. Hulme realised, however, that the assault on the pa was hopeless, and a general retreat was sounded. Hulme's army left the field.

News of a great British victory was spread around the country — a view that does not stand up to close analysis. Kawiti had learned a valuable lesson. Although he had stopped the assault on the pa, he did so at a heavy cost. After the battle about 30 anti-government Maori lay dead and another 50 were wounded. British casualties were 14 killed and 40 wounded.

This was to be the first and last time the Maori would face the British on open ground on this scale. They would very quickly find new ways of fighting.

TE AHUAHU

After the battle of Puketutu Heke abandoned the pa and returned to Te Ahuahu a short distance away. It was here that Waka Nene attacked Heke without the assistance of the British. Details of this event are a bit sketchy but it seems that this battle was fought in a more traditional Maori manner, in the open, and involved around 500 combatants. Waka Nene got the upper hand in this fight and Heke was wounded and came close to being taken prisoner. This was to be the only defeat Heke was to suffer throughout the Northern War, as we shall see, and although the British authorities were slow in recognising Waka Nene's efforts, they were quick to move on the advantage it presented them. While Heke was licking his wounds, they planned to strike and crush the rebels. Unfortunately for the British, this wasn't to be.

OHAEAWAI

The roads up north these days are obviously a lot better than they were 140 years ago. It's hard to believe that the British took all day to travel from the mission station at Waimate to Ohaeawai. I did the same trip in my clapped-out but noble Mk 4 Cortina in under 15 minutes. Mind you, I chose not to go in the middle of winter and I had a change of clothing and a Visa card.

According to my calculations the Ohaeawai battle site was on State Highway 12 between Ohaeawai and Kaikohe. I shot off down SH12 from Ohaeawai expecting to come across the place any second. When I didn't find it right away, I started to think I had another search on my hands. I decided to turn back, thinking I must have passed it already. I pulled into a driveway to turn around and was greeted by a signpost that told me I was there.

It's an incredibly beautiful place. The driveway from the road winds around a small hill, on top of which sits an old and beautiful church surrounded by a graveyard and a stone wall. I was brought up a Christian but I guess the rope kind'a broke, but I would have been happy to attend a service there. It's that kind of place.

The story of what happened there in June and July of 1845 also stands out in my mind as one of the most significant battles fought in New Zealand, and the ground that I now stood on was the scene of some tragic and desperate tales.

The graveyard is a mixture of old and new graves, including a mass grave holding the bodies of British soldiers who died while fighting there. They were originally buried behind the British camp, but were moved to the churchyard and laid out by the Maori after peace was made. The bodies of Maori chiefs are also there; and if there was such a thing as a list of 'most interesting graveyards' you would not have to go down it too far before you found Ohaeawai. In spite of this I felt uncomfortable about taking photographs in the graveyard

Te Ahuahu.

itself. The stone wall surrounding the church and graveyard sits on the same boundary as the original stockade built by Kawiti.

Colonel Despard, recently arrived from Sydney, was in charge of the 99th and 58th Regiments. Despard had had considerable active service in India and was considered to be a competent leader, but he was not at all familiar with New Zealand, and was fighting a foe whom he greatly underestimated. He also failed to take full advantage of the advice of his Maori allies under Waka Nene.

Despard sailed across the bay from Kororareka to Kerikeri and from there set out for the mission station at Waimate some 12 miles away. The 600-odd men under his command included soldiers from the 58th, 96th, 99th, 75 men from the Auckland Militia and 18 from the HMS *Hazard*. Things started badly and only got worse. The men struggled to get several pieces of artillery, ammunition and other supplies over very bad roads that were quickly churned to mud in the Northland winter. The column broke

Waimate Mission Station Church.

up under these conditions and it wasn't until the next day that they all reassembled at Waimate. There Despard was approached by Waka Nene with an offer to assist in the operations. Despard's response was that when he wanted the help of savages he would ask for it — and it was only the quick thinking of an interpreter which avoided a situation that could have meant the loss of Waka Nene and his 300 men.

They stayed at Waimate for a couple of days waiting for fresh supplies to be brought up from Kerikeri, then set off for Kawiti's pa at Ohaeawai, arriving there on 23 June 1845. Waka Nene's advance guard were the first to come under fire as they skirmished their way into position, and Despard's main camp was set up about 500 yards from the pa. Waka Nene set up camp on the top of Puketapu Hill, 600 yards from the pa, and from there he was able to see into Kawiti's position and could thus provide security for Despard's forces.

It was at Ohaeawai that Kawiti came close to fulfilling his vow to kill 100 British soldiers. He built his pa with modifications specifically designed for fighting the British army. Inside the pa were bombproof shelters to protect the inhabitants during shelling, and the firing trenches just behind the palisade were built in sections so as to prevent enfilading fire (the enemy firing straight down the trench from one end to the other). The sections were joined by small communication trenches (saps) that enabled the garrison to move freely from one part of the pa to another. Outside the main palisade and running about three feet from it was another lighter fence — a pekerangi. This was designed to slow down an advancing party, giving the occupants an opportunity to shoot them as they clambered over. Also from the palisade hung huge flax mats, the purpose of which was twofold. First, they were virtually musket-proof, giving the defenders almost total protection; and second, as a cannonball went through the mat, the mat would close up, so that the attackers had no view of the damage it may have caused. These modifications were to prove successful, and the pa at Ohaeawai was the first of many of its type to be built throughout the New Zealand Wars.

On 24 June the bombardment began. It was to last six days. It was a trying time — Despard had thought the whole operation would take only three days, and food supplies for the troops were running short. For several days the only food ration was half a pound of flour per man per day, mixed into damper and cooked over a fire. In addition they received quarter of a pint of rum at break of day and again in the evening. The soldiers were constantly wet and exposed to the elements, and were growing weaker.

In spite of the fact that 400 shells were fired at the pa during the first couple of days, no significant breach was made. Kawiti had positioned himself within a short distance of the bush, and extra timber could easily be brought into the pa for repairs, carried out during the frequent lapses in bombardment. Despard decided that a breach would have

John Williams' watercolour of the action at Ohaeawai. Alexander Turnbull Library F-754-1/1.

Ohaeawai, showing the stone wall that sits on the same boundary as the original stockade built by Kawiti.

to be forced by means of an assault. Someone had the brilliant idea of constructing shields of flax, to be carried in front of the storming parties to protect them from musket fire from the pa. Despard approved the plan, and ordered the shields to be made in time for the assault, which was to be carried out at night. Many of the officers and men considered the plan to be ludicrous, and were relieved when the assault was called off due to bad weather. It was only after the cancellation that the flax screens were tested: shots were fired at them, and they proved to be less than bulletproof.

Another scheme hatched by the officers of the artillery was to fill the empty shell cases with some poisonous and foul-smelling substance, attach a short fuse and fire them into the pa's compound. This plan was carried out, with no effect whatsoever on the physical health of the pa's defenders. (The mind boggles as to what the substance may have been.)

The shelling continued and still no breach was made. Colonel Despard therefore ordered a 32-pounder to be brought up from the *Hazard* and, in the meantime, ordered another assault. The officers under his command realised that an assault at this stage would cost too many lives, and the increasingly impatient Despard was talked out of it. On 30 June a bullock team dragged the heavy gun into camp, under intense fire from the pa, and positioned it on the slopes of Puketapu.

Work on the gun's position was carried out during the night, but in the morning, before it could be brought into use, part of Kawiti's garrison launched a surprise attack on Waka Nene's position at the top of the hill. Waka Nene and his followers were caught unawares and fled down the hill to the main camp. At the time Despard was directing the work at the gun position, and he and his men were swept up in the general retreat and also forced to retire. Upon reaching the main camp, a now furious Despard ordered a counterattack and the hilltop was easily retaken. Kawiti's men, upon reaching the safety of the pa, raised a Union Jack taken in the raid; and this flag as well as an item of Maori clothing fluttering from the flagpole were the last straw for Despard. Without waiting to see the effects of the 32-pounder he ordered an assault. If Kawiti's raid and the subsequent flag-flying episode were designed to induce an assault before the big gun could be used against them, it was a ploy that worked like a charm.

The assault on Ohaeawai has been compared to the Crimean 'Charge of the Light Brigade', although I have to wonder if the Crimean charge was a sound and reasonable decision by comparison. The assault party was made up of a little over 250 men, divided into two main groups, plus an advance party of about 20. These men advanced on the pa, initially using what cover they could find, and then charged over the last 50 yards. Upon reaching the outer pekerangi they came under an awesome volley from the pa which, according to one of the defenders, had men falling 'like sticks being thrown on the ground'.

This volley was followed up by independent firing, as the attackers tried to pull down the stockade with their swords and bare hands. They could not see a single Maori, as they were safe in trenches behind the palisade.

Ladders were brought up with the assault party by members of the Auckland Militia, but only one was put up the side of the wall. To climb it would have meant certain death — as was proved by one sailor. Within seven minutes two men out of every five who took part in the assault were either killed or wounded. In spite of this they did not retreat until ordered to do so by Colonel Despard himself. Lieutenant Philpotts, leading the naval detachment and possibly trying to redeem himself after the sacking of Kororareka, ran along the outside of the wall trying to find a way in and, on climbing the palisade, was killed. The soldiers thought they had to take the pa or die in the attempt, and when the first retreat was sounded on the bugle they thought it was a mistake. Eventually it was sounded again and they left the field carrying what wounded they could, many of them returning to rescue more.

After the battle the dead were collected under a flag of truce. The bodies of the rank and file were buried at Ohaeawai and the officers at the Waimate mission, where their graves can still be visited today. Two days after the charge Kawiti and the Maori garrison abandoned the pa and Colonel Despard claimed victory, and once again everybody blamed everybody else for the disastrous assault.

There was to be no more fighting until the attack on Ruapekapeka five months later.

RUAPEKAPEKA

When I left Auckland and headed up north I was full of anticipation. I had read a good deal about Ruapekapeka and Ohaeawai and the attack on Kororareka and I looked forward to standing on the ground where all this had happened.

The weather had looked promising when I left Auckland, but as I travelled north the clouds turned up and became heavier. The quality of the light was diminishing, and rain was looking likely. I thought I would go to the site anyway, even if I didn't end up taking any photos. I had no trouble finding it — it was right where the map said it would be, in the middle of nowhere. I climbed up the path past the Department of Conservation signposts, and there I was.

The sign at the gate says Ruapekapeka is a sacred place — and it is. I have visited places of spiritual importance in Hawaii and Arizona in the United States, and the atmosphere of those places is the same as it is here and in many other spots throughout the country. Quiet, still, and yet very much alive.

The first things I noticed as I walked onto Ruapekapeka were a cannon, and a Maori carving mounted at the centre of the site. The carving, although old and weatherbeaten, looked down on the site with an imposing presence. At first glance the cannon looked as though it had simply been left behind after the battle. It was one of two that Kawiti had at the pa; and in the course of the battle it received a direct hit and was smashed. The pieces have been put back together and now stand as an effective monument to the battle of Ruapekapeka.

All over the site were rifle pits, which were partially blocked so as to prevent enfilading fire. Bombproof bunkers were still plainly visible, and in some cases were big enough to fall into — walking backwards at Ruapekapeka is not to be recommended.

The site was fantastic: the light for taking photographs was not. Also, I felt uneasy about photographing the carving, unless I had permission to do so. I decided to come back later.

No sooner had I thought this than I felt the sun on my back and, looking up, I saw a small break in the clouds overhead. I had been told to look out for omens while I was travelling around the East Coast. To me, this appeared to be a good one.

On 7 December 1845 over 1000 British troops under the command of Colonel Despard and their Maori allies under the command of Waka Nene assembled at the Kawakawa River and advanced from there to attack Kawiti's pa at Ruapekapeka. They had to cover 18 miles of rugged country, over a road that they built as they went. With them they took 30 tons of artillery, and each man was required to carry a shell, weighing up to 32 pounds, in addition to his own gun and equipment. It was three weeks before the entire force was assembled before the pa.

As the advance guard approached, Kawiti's men left the pa and attacked but were forced back. Despard lost no time in setting up three battery positions and protecting them with a series of strong stockades. The bombardment of the pa began, and was kept up for two weeks. On 10 January Hone Heke and his followers joined Kawiti, bringing the numbers defending the pa to about 500.

The bombardment was starting to take its toll on the palisade around the pa, although the garrison inside was protected within the bombproof shelters. Heke and Kawiti decided to abandon the pa and to lure the British into the surrounding bush where they could not take the big guns, and where positions had been prepared for an ambush.

The following day it was reported to Despard that groups of Maori could be seen leaving the pa, carrying food and other supplies with them. An assault was ordered and Captain Denny and 100 men of the 58th Regiment charged the pa and entered through a breach made by the bombardment. Inside the pa at the time were Kawiti and a handful of warriors, who gave one last volley and fled outside to join Heke and the rest of the garrison.

The plan to lure the British into the bush was only partly successful. Some of the

The remains of one of Kawiti's cannons at the site of Ruapekapeka.

The British encampment at Ruapekapeka. Alexander Turnbull Library F-30266-1/2.

58th went into the bush, and these men suffered heavy casualties, but the bulk of the force remained where they were, and many used the pa as their own defence position. The initial assault on the pa was launched in the morning, and the fight that followed lasted until about two o'clock in the afternoon, when Kawiti and Heke withdrew from the field of battle, having prolonged the fight as long as possible in order to evacuate the wounded. The British forces withdrew from Ruapekapeka, leaving behind a lot of equipment and supplies, and during their march back to the coast they were under constant threat of attack.

This was to be the last battle of the Northern War. A week later Kawiti and Heke let it be known that they desired peace, and the new governor, Grey, realising that he did not have the means to crush the rebellion, turned necessity into virtue and granted them that peace. The first war between European and Maori was over and, as it was to be with subsequent wars in this country, the result was inconclusive. Hone Heke and Kawiti had won the battles at Kororareka, Puketutu and Ohaeawai. Waka Nene had won at Te Ahuahu, and the closest the British came to a victory was at Ruapekapeka, though how much of a victory it was is still being debated. Heke's and Kawiti's forces were still intact but nothing had been won or lost in real terms — life just returned to the way it was before the fighting had started. The flagstaff on Maiki Hill, the symbol of discontent, was not raised again until after the death of Hone Heke in 1850.

The First Taranaki War

It amazes me how quickly the Maori got around this country in days of old. When the Waikato Maori went to fight alongside those in Taranaki they would go up the Waikato and Waipa Rivers, cross the ranges, go down the Mokau River to the sea and then follow the coastline to Waitara and beyond. The whole trip would take two days.

I had never been to the mouth of the Mokau River and wanted to check it out. When I got there it was September and the whitebaiters were out in force with their nets. The surrounding beach was covered with heavy chunks of driftwood. It was cold, but that didn't seem to bother anyone as they waded in the water, sweeping their nets in an effort to catch the tiny delicacy. I stopped and chatted to a woman who was there with her family, and she spoke of the delights of spending a day wandering about in cold water hoping to get enough for a feed when they got back home. As we passed the time of day her daughter called out, 'Mum, I got one,' and she replied, 'Good on ya, girl.' I wished her luck and said I hoped that she would get enough for a good dinner. 'Oh, I never eat the stuff,' she said. 'I'm allergic to eggs so I can't eat the batter. I'll be giving these to my neighbour.'

It was about five o'clock when I drove into Waitara. I was hungry and needed a place to sleep. The town centre was quiet — things had wound down for the day. Spotting a hotel, I went to push the door open but found it locked. I have a standing joke with a good mate of mine — we have decided that if ever we have enough money to buy a pub we'll lock the doors, and if anybody turns up for a drink we'll tell them to go and buy their own pub. Could it be that I had found someone who had fulfilled our dream?

I went to the bottlestore next door and the chap there made a phone call on my behalf. He told me the owner had a room and would let me in if I went 'round to the side door'. I bought a six-pack, for research purposes, and found the pub owner waiting for me. He showed me to my room. It was huge and had a good view of the town; and it had a TV — but no aerial. 'Hang on,' he said and disappeared. A moment later he returned, aerial in hand.

'I got this from my wife's set. She won't mind.' I figured that if she did, I would soon find out.

On his recommendation I went across the road to the local restaurant-cum-takeaway bar and bought the best steak burger I have ever had. I went back to my room and settled down to a bit of research, with the TV on.

I had a plastic bag full of maps, courtesy of the Automobile Association (when you drive a car like mine it pays to be a member), and pulling out the street map of Waitara I made a curious discovery. Virtually every street in Waitara is named after a British officer or a government official from the 1860s. Nowhere is there a Wiremu Kingi Street or a Hapurona Avenue. These were extraordinary people, and as Waitara grows, I hope they will be remembered.

Wiremu Kingi was the paramount chief of Te Atiawa whose tribal lands were in Waitara and the surrounding area. He had once stated that he loved the Europeans, and indeed he had assisted them during the outbreak of violence in the Wellington area in 1847. In return for his services Kingi was held in high regard by the Europeans, but this diminished as the pressure to sell tribal land to settlers increased. The land in question was owned by the tribe as a whole and could not be sold without the consent of all, and as paramount chief Wiremu Kingi had the right to veto any attempted purchase.

Kingi, however, was embroiled in a dispute with another Te Atiawa chief by the name of Te Teira. At the centre of the dispute was a woman called Hariata, who was married to one Ihaia Te Kiri-kumara. Hariata had an affair with a man called Rimene, and in an act of revenge, Rimene was killed by Ihaia. Ihaia then sought further compensation, but the people of the tribe felt that the insult had been avenged and enough was enough.

Panoramic view from the site of the Omata redoubt overlooking Waireka.

Ihaia joined forces with Te Teira, who owed money to the government agent, Robert Reid Parris, and so was keen to sell land himself. As a way of airing the grievance, Te Teira offered to sell a block of land, about 600 acres, to the government. Wiremu Kingi opposed the sale and everybody, including the advisers to the recently appointed Governor Thomas Gore Browne, knew that the deal was shaky, to say the least. In spite of this the governor allowed the purchase to proceed and on 20 February 1860, surveyors arrived on the disputed land and started to mark out some 980 acres.

The surveyors were met with resistance, and boundary pegs were pulled out. There was no violence — in fact the occasion was good natured, although the surveyors were sent back to New Plymouth. Wiremu Kingi was hoping that those involved in pulling out the surveyors' pegs would be arrested and that the whole matter would be brought before a British court of law in order to expose the injustice of the land deal, but the British authorities did not oblige.

In the meantime Parris had announced the land title clear for purchase (which was blatantly untrue), and Te Teira received his first down-payment of 100 pounds — which, coincidentally, was the exact amount that he owed Parris.

Lt-Colonel G. Murray sent a message to Wiremu Kingi stating that further obstruction of the surveyors would be considered an act of rebellion and that he was prepared to send in the troops to occupy the land in question if need be. Wiremu Kingi had no wish to fight the Pakeha — up until recently he had regarded them as his friends. In his reply to Murray he stated, 'Is that your love for me, to bring soldiers to Waitara? This is not love, it is anger. I do not wish for love, all I want is the land.'

Martial law was declared, and on 5 March 1860 the British army occupied Waitara,

Wiremu Kingi. Taranaki Museum.

setting up a camp that was to remain the base of their operations for the next 12 months. As the troops moved in, Te Atiawa fled. They watched from a distance as the troops, assisted by Maori loyal to the Queen, burnt homes and crops.

Te Atiawa now had no choice but to fight a war they had never wanted. The first confrontation was not a big affair, but it was to serve as a warm-up for some serious killing that was to follow.

Wiremu Kingi and his war chief Hapurona built a pa at Te Kohia. This pa, also known as the 'L-pa' because of its unusual shape, was built in a night — and, from a strategic point of view, was totally expendable. Bombproof bunkers were constructed inside the walls of the pa. The importance of these shelters appears to have been lost on Colonel Gold, who stated in his report that the pa had been 'curiously hollowed out'.

On 17 March 1860 Colonel Gold attacked the pa with three companies of the 65th Regiment, a few sailors from HMS *Niger*, 20 men from the Royal Artillery with three field guns, and 20 men from the volunteer cavalry. The guns opened fire from 750 yards away and were moved closer and closer as the day went on. As they moved within rifle range of the pa they came under fire from the garrison inside the pa — less than 100 men. The artillery was accurate, with nearly every shell finding its mark, and the flagpole with the war flag flying from the pa was hit and hung over the palisade. A group of volunteer cavalry rode up to the pa, and after emptying their revolvers into it, made away with the flag. They received a volley for their trouble and one of them, John Sarten, aged 22 years, fell from his horse dead, earning the dubious distinction of being the first man killed in the Taranaki War.

Shots were exchanged throughout the night, but by morning the British found the pa abandoned. In spite of the hefty bombardment, Wiremu Kingi and his followers had escaped without losing a single man. The imperial army had captured a now useless pa and the only prisoner taken was a dog found wandering around the devastated interior.

Within ten days another drama was to unfold, this time at Waireka, five miles south of New Plymouth.

Since the outbreak of hostilities, settlers from the area surrounding New Plymouth had begun to abandon their farms and move to the safety of the New Plymouth settlement. Te Atiawa were being reinforced by the tribes of Southern Taranaki, and farmhouses were being burned and livestock driven off. On 27 March five settlers were murdered, and when the news arrived in New Plymouth the next day it was decided to rescue the remaining settlers in the Waireka and Omata District. The principal concern was for the Rev. H.H. Brown and his family, although the Maori had stated that, because of his position, the Reverend would be protected. The other settlers in the immediate area were French and Portuguese and there was little concern for their safety, as the Maori had also made it clear that their fight was with the British only.

The expeditionary force that moved out of New Plymouth on 28 March was split into two groups. The first was made up of the Taranaki Rifle Volunteers and Militia, about 160 men in all, under the command of Captain Charles Brown. Their objective was to move out along the beach to Waireka and gather up the 'stranded' settlers and then join up with Lt-Colonel Murray and 88 men from the 65th Regiment and 25 from the Royal Navy (off the *Niger*), who were to go to Waireka via the Devon Road. Murray was expecting to engage a 'rebel' force at Omata, but when he arrived there was none to be seen, and he continued his advance at a leisurely pace.

The colonial militia went along the beach and up the Waireka Stream, where they were spotted by Maori from the Kaipopo Pa who streamed out of the pa and fired on them. The fighting that followed was heavy and Captain Brown, who had no previous experience of soldiering, passed his command to Captain Stapp, who had fought as a corporal in the 58th Regiment against Hone Heke. The Maori from the Kaipopo Pa continued along the Waireka Stream and threatened to cut off the beach route back to New Plymouth. Captain Stapp moved his force to the farmhouse at Jurys' farm and fortified the place with fenceposts and railings and anything else that came to hand.

Lt-Colonel Murray arrived, and upon hearing the rifle fire, sent a detachment to link up with the militia. In order to keep the route to New Plymouth open he also sent out skirmishes, as well as firing rockets at Kaipopo Pa. He was under orders to return to New Plymouth before dark: the settlement was in a state of siege and under constant threat of attack, and was vulnerable without the protection of the soldiers. Whether Murray fully understood the plight of the militia or not is hard to say, but as night began to fall

The monument to the Maori Wars on top of Marsland Hill, New Plymouth.

Marsland Hill barracks in the centre of New Plymouth, built to protect the city and the settlers from Taranaki farms who moved in to escape the wars. Taranaki Museum.

he sounded the recall of his troops and made his way back to New Plymouth. In doing so, he abandoned the colonial troops in their hour of need.

It is hard to estimate the amount of danger the militia were in. Certainly it must have seemed to them that they were in serious trouble. Ammunition was running short, so Stapp made sure each man had at least one spare round for when the rush came, after which they would rely on the bayonet.

Help was, however, on the way from an unexpected quarter. Back at New Plymouth Captain Cracroft of the *Niger* had received reports of the fighting and, with the permission of Colonel Gold, had moved out of New Plymouth with 60 of his men with the intention of attacking the pa at Kaipopo. As he approached he spotted the flag flying from the pa, and told his men that he would pay 10 pounds to the man who brought it down. His sailors rushed the pa and took it. The initial reports stated that there were up to 150 Maori who put up a desperate fight; but it now seems certain the pa was empty except for one or two men, too old to fight. The sailor who took the flag was the Captain's coxswain, William Odgers, who later received the Victoria Cross for this action as well as getting the 10 pounds. Not a bad day's work.

The attack on the pa had the effect, however, of forcing the Maori to withdraw and leave the battlefield empty. Captain Brown and Captain Stapp gathered up the dead and wounded, about a dozen in all, and were back in New Plymouth by midnight.

Estimates of Maori casualties range from 17 to 50, depending on which account you choose to believe.

PUKETAKAUERE

The colonial government was well aware that Wiremu Kingi was lobbying the tribes of the Waikato region for their support. In June 1858 a huge meeting was held in the Waikato, organised by the Ngati Haua chief Wiremu Tamehana, at which the land was placed under the authority of the great Waikato chief Te Wherowhero in an effort to protect it from further alienation. Te Wherowhero was pronounced King, and the King Movement was born. Te Wherowhero, or King Potatau (meaning 'he who watches at night') as he was called after his investiture, died in 1860 and was succeeded by his son Tawhiao. Not wanting to give the Kingites an easy excuse to join in the fighting in Taranaki, Governor Browne ordered a suspension of hostilities against Te Atiawa. This cessation was to last from 20 April to 23 June. Te Atiawa, however, had stated to Tawhiao that the land 'purchase' in Waitara was unjust; and they also stressed that they had sworn allegiance to the King Movement. In spite of efforts on the part of the colonial government to dissuade the Kingites from doing so, they decided to send war parties to Taranaki to fight alongside Te Atiawa.

The Taranaki and Waikato tribes, who for a long time were enemies, were now united by a common foe, the British.

Te Atiawa, sensing an opportunity for victory, lost no time in preparing for battle. Fortifications were prepared about a mile from the British military camp at Waitara, a distance that was too close for the imperial troops to ignore. The Maori defences were on two hills — Onukukaitara, on which they built a new stockade; and Puketakauere, which appeared to have little or no defences. These two hills rested between two swampy gullies that formed a V-shape pointing towards the Waitara River. The hills were garrisoned with less than 200 men under the command of Te Atiawa war chief Hapurona.

There were a few extraordinary Maori generals who were to emerge from the history of these times, and Hapurona was certainly one of them. He had chosen the time and the place for this battle, on ground that appeared to the British to be easy to take. A British reconnaissance party approached the pa on 23 June and was fired on. If they needed an excuse for the suspension of hostilities to be called off, this was it.

Major Nelson had at his disposal 350 men, which he apparently felt was more than enough to take the Maori position. He divided his men into three groups. The first, under the command of Captain Messenger, was of 125 men. Their job was to take Puketakauere from the rear and cut off any Maori retreat in that direction. In order for them to do this it was necessary to get into position during the night — a difficult task, due to the swampy terrain.

The main group of 180 men, under the command of Major Nelson, was to force a breach in the stockade on Onukukaitara and then attack across the open ground in front. Another 50 men, under Captain Bowdler, were to take up position between the pa and the camp at Waitara, thus cutting off another avenue for escape. Major Nelson opened fire with two howitzers at seven o'clock and when these two 24-pounders had done their work, he advanced his men across open ground towards the defences of Onukukaitara as planned.

What wasn't planned was the fact that within the pa there were very few Maori warriors, as Hapurona had deployed most of his force in hidden trenches and rifle pits well in front of the pa itself. So in effect Nelson's bombardment had been aimed at a false target. When the advance of Nelson's men came close enough they suddenly found themselves in an ambush from a position they did not know existed. The first volley from the Maori checked the British advance, and as Nelson rallied his men to continue, extra support for the Maori came as more men arrived from the pa to join the fighting from the rifle pits and the natural gully that formed the Maori defence. Nelson came under heavy fire again and was forced to retreat. Captain Messenger found himself in the same situation, but his troubles were compounded by the difficult

The British camp at Waitara. Alexander Turnbull Library F-624-1/1.

Puketakauere Pa site.

terrain. His force soon became fragmented and retreated. Messenger arrived at camp at about the same time as Nelson, only to have Nelson send him back to look for more of his men. The whole retreat was covered by Lieutenant McNaughten's howitzers with a steady fire of case shot.

By 11 am it was all over, apart from stragglers making their way back to camp. Many of the wounded were left on the field or in the swamps, and few of these survived the fury of the battle. The British casualties were 30 killed and 34 wounded, and Maori losses were no more than five.

MAHOETAHI

The only tribe from the Waikato allowed by King Potatau to fight alongside the Taranaki Maori at the battle of Puketakauere were the Ngati Maniapoto. After his death, and with the Maori victory at Puketakauere, support for the cause grew among all the Waikato tribes. There was no stopping them — they were spoiling for a fight.

The Taranaki were fighting for the land they lived on: to maintain control of the land was to control their own destiny. At this stage of the war the Waikato Maori were fighting the British in order to protect themselves against European domination. Not long before the Taranaki War, the Waikato and Taranaki tribes had been enemies. In the early 1830s Te Atiawa were invaded by tribes from the Waikato, and a major battle was fought at the ancient pa of Pukerangiora, a little distance to the south of Huirangi. After a long siege the Waikato captured the pa and killed about 1200 people. Many others chose to throw themselves off the clifftop into the Waitara River 90 metres below. Many slaves were taken, including Te Atiawa war chief Hapurona. For these two peoples to unite against a common foe, the threat must have been very real.

Warriors from all over the Waikato massed at Kihikihi and travelled to Taranaki to fight. At first Te Atiawa were reluctant to fight another battle, but they agreed to allow the Waikato warriors, led by Wetini Taiporutu, to make a stand on a small hill at Mahoetahi.

I had never seen the Mahoetahi site, but something was telling me that it would be a beautiful place. It is, and it's also a sad place. There are a lot of brave people buried there.

It lies on the Devon Road between Waitara and New Plymouth, and as you climb up the rise you soon forget about the noise from the traffic below. The site consists of a fence, a cross marking the grave of 36 people who died there, a tree, and a sign giving some information about what happened there. On the sign is a copy of a painting depicting a battle, but they've got it wrong — the painting is a scene from the battle of Te Ngutu-o-te-Manu, fought 10 years later, not Mahoetahi.

I'm no military expert, but this site does not appear to me to be one that could easily be defended. At the time of the battle the hill was virtually surrounded by swamp, which has since been drained, and this may have slowed down an attacking force; but in spite of this the hill itself seems too low and too small to be used as a defensive position, especially when compared to other more successful battle sites.

Wetini Taiporutu and about 130 warriors, some Te Atiawa but mostly members of the Waikato King Movement, crossed the Waitara River on 5 November 1860 and entrenched at Mahoetahi, having sent a challenge to the military at New Plymouth.

Command by this stage had passed to Major General Pratt, who coincidentally was planning to take immediate possession of Mahoetahi, and was in a position to respond to the challenge. The next day he marched on the hill with a total of 650 men from the 65th, 40th and 12th Regiments, the Taranaki Rifle Volunteers and Militia, and the volunteer cavalry. With the force were about 100 Maori loyal to the Queen, but when the fighting started they refused to participate.

Pratt had organised a rendezvous with Colonel Mould (65th) and Major Nelson (40th) from Camp Waitara with their own detachments, and took up position on the

The low hill of Mahoetahi.

north side of the hill, while Pratt's forces came along the Devon Road and set up the artillery and lines of attack from the south.

Wetini Taiporutu was having breakfast when the alarm was sounded. He continued to sit quietly, finishing his meal, until he received the news that the pa was surrounded. It was to be his last meal.

Captain Atkinson of the Taranaki Volunteers and his men led the attack. They skirted the west side of the pa, eventually turning the Maori flank, while the 65th approached the pa directly in front, from the south. As they approached they received a volley from inside the pa, but it would appear that the Maori may have fired too soon, as this inflicted very little damage. Using the cover of two low hills and the surrounding swamp, Atkinson's rifle volunteers managed to get into the pa without losing a man, although two were killed in the close fighting that followed.

Wetini was supposed to have been reinforced by Te Atiawa led by Hapurona, but they fired their guns from a distance then left the scene. Possibly they were cut off from the action by the arrival of Colonel Mould's 65th and Nelson's 40th from Waitara; or their non-involvement may have been due to some sort of internal politics. Whatever the reason, it left Wetini Taiporutu with too few men to defend the pa. Once Atkinson's men got into the pa the 65th charged with renewed vigour and the Maori garrison was forced to retreat and make off towards Huirangi in the east.

Mould and Nelson then released their men to take up the chase, and the Maori, who were outnumbered, began to suffer heavy casualties. It was reported that in their effort to get away they abandoned guns, ammunition and anything else that would slow them down. Most escaped, but the British and colonial troops could now claim a victory — though of little real value. Wetini Taiporutu and 50 or so of his men were killed, and about the same number wounded. Thirty-six of them are buried in a mass grave on the west side of the Mahoetahi Hill.

TE AREI

If you're ever in Taranaki and have an urge to wander around a battle site, pay a visit to Te Arei. It's a dramatic place. It's also on farm land, and when I was there I had plenty of sheep to keep me company. I was careful not to disturb them.

To get there, follow the Waitara Road that runs to the right of the Waitara River, travelling east. You will know you're getting close as you pass signs that indicate the position of the redoubts that were built on the way — there were eight of them.

Eventually you'll find Te Arei Pa. Below it, on the flat, are the remains of the sap, complete with traverses every few yards to prevent enfilading fire. Another trench at right angles to the main sap extends 60 metres to the left. This demi-parallel was used to attack rifle pits built by the defenders. At the end of this trench is the spot where Lieutenant McNaughten, the man who fired the first shot in the Taranaki War, was killed — exactly one year later.

Climb to the top of the hill and you're on Te Arei. Te Arei means 'the barrier' and that is exactly what it was. It was a fighting pa designed to protect the ancient pa of Pukerangiora directly behind it. Trenches and rifle pits are still plainly visible at Te Arei and the view from the cliffs looking over the Waitara River is spectacular and disturbing, considering the events of long ago.

Te Atiawa, assisted by tribes from the Waikato, built a series of pa as a defence line ultimately protecting Pukerangiora. Major-General Pratt proposed to attack these pa by building a series of redoubts, each a short distance from the next, until he had his own defence line going right up to Pukerangiora. Instead of the British attacking each pa, using unreliable methods, the Maori would be forced to attack the redoubts, thus drawing them out into the open. Colonial troops were not invited to attend this campaign, as they were thought too undisciplined for this type of work — they were left to defend New Plymouth.

The township of New Plymouth had been under siege for a long time. Life there was not easy: farmers from the outlying area had moved in for safety, the town was becoming overcrowded, and disease had broken out. Maori raiding parties from outside the town were burning houses and driving off livestock, threatening to destroy the local economy. (These raids were at least partly in revenge for the destruction of Maori crops and housing by the imperial and colonial forces.)

When Pratt and his staff announced their plan, it was ridiculed by the settlers at New Plymouth — they thought it too slow and too cautious. Many of the Maori had heard about it too, and they also thought the whole thing was a bit of a joke, and offered to dig the flying sap for the British themselves at a shilling per man per day. Hapurona, though, took the threat seriously and started to make sure his own defences were ready.

With the camp at Waitara as a base for operations, the campaign started on 29 December 1860. Before daybreak Pratt's forces moved out and, sending out skirmishers to keep the Maori defenders at bay, built the first of the redoubts, about 1000 yards west of the Matarikoriko Pa. While the redoubt was being built artillery opened up on the pa. From all accounts the fighting that day must have been heavy — by 6 pm, when the outer walls were finished, the British army had fired 70,000 rounds of ammunition and 120 shells. Three men had been killed and another 21 wounded. The redoubt was garrisoned with a detachment of the 40th Regiment while the rest of the force went back to Waitara.

The following day was Sunday and when the missionary Wilson went to Matarikoriko to deliver a service, he returned with the news that the pa had been abandoned. Before the Maori could reoccupy it Pratt moved onto the site and built another redoubt and garrisoned it. The first pa in the Maori line of defence had fallen.

The second and third redoubts on a line towards Te Arei were built in the same manner as the first, each 400–500 yards apart. As Pratt's forces approached Huirangi, resistance from the defenders increased, and No. 3 redoubt became the base for the digging of a sap.

The sap was a trench, dug at about 60 yards a day towards the Maori position, so that the troops could advance under cover. The sap was reinforced with gabions — baskets made of flax and supplejack, filled with earth and fern to make them bulletproof. At the head of the sap was one of these baskets, the sap roller, which was pushed forward as the work progressed. The sap roller was booby-trapped at night with an artillery shell attached to a friction fuse. A raid carried out on the sap one night left two men badly injured.

Work on the sap began on 22 January, and that night Hapurona, Rewi Maniapoto and Epiha and 140 hand-picked men attacked the No. 3 redoubt. These men, supported by another 200 who were positioned in the surrounding fern and had the job of shooting any soldier who showed himself above the parapet, crept into the trench surrounding the redoubt. Once there they tried, unsuccessfully, to scale the walls of the redoubt, and some who were without guns leapt up, slashing with their tomahawks and trying to pull the guns from the soldiers' hands as they fired down into the trench.

At the time the redoubt was garrisoned by 450 men under the command of Lt-Colonel Leslie, and these men lost no time in attaching short fuses to some artillery shells and rolled them into the ditches. The shells exploded, killing and maiming many, but it was not until the garrison from No. 1 redoubt led a counterattack that the Maori withdrew, leaving behind some 50 dead, as well as about 30 guns, various mere and other weapons.

The Maori had attacked No. 3 redoubt thinking that it would be lightly manned, but it would appear that there had been a tip-off. The Maori had lost the battle at Mahoetahi, but the defeat was due to a mixture of bad planning and bad luck. The attack on No. 3 redoubt was a blunder — one of the few mistakes the Maori made in the Taranaki War.

The sap advanced slowly. Every 10–12 yards it was partially blocked, to prevent anybody shooting down its length. The soldiers found the work frustrating and would rather have had an open attack but the commanding officers did not give them the chance. Along the sap line, redoubts Nos 4, 5, 6, and 7 were built. The defenders of Huirangi had fallen back on Te Arei and from No. 7 redoubt the British, having brought up extra artillery, commenced to bombard it.

By March 1861, No. 8 redoubt was built and the sap pushed forward, with the soldiers

Te Arie Pa site.

Sap approaching Te Arie.

The Te Arie sap in 1896. Taranaki Museum.

coming under intense fire from a series of rifle pits to the left. To flush these out a demi-parallel was dug, about 67 yards long.

Wiremu Tamehana had come down from the Waikato in an effort to negotiate peace, and for three days hostilities and sap-digging were suspended while the talks were held. Pratt, who by this stage had gone to a lot of trouble, refused to agree to Tamehana's proposal for a cessation of hostilities and a return to the status quo. On 15 March the fighting resumed, until a white flag was shown from Te Arei on 19 March. By this time the sap was 1626 yards long and, in spite of the fact that it was considered a safe way to go, British casualties numbered about 80. The Maori casualties were about 100.

Unlike General Pratt, Governor Browne was willing to talk peace with Te Atiawa, and sent the Native Secretary Donald McLean to negotiate a ceasefire. Under the terms of this agreement the British demanded the return of all plunder taken during the raids (none was returned). They also insisted that any Maori who had murdered an unarmed civilian in the course of these raids be handed over to British justice (none was handed over). Hapurona was given custody of the redoubt at Matarikoriko and put on a salary of 100 pounds per year, in the hope that this would keep him from any more fighting, and Wiremu Kingi retired to the King Country in self-imposed exile. Even as this peace was being negotiated the last of the livestock was being driven off farms surrounding the besieged town of New Plymouth and the Maori still had control of Tataraimaka. In effect the settlers had control over less land that they had before the start of the war; and they were pretty dubious about the so-called peace agreement. But the colonial authorities realised that there was little to be gained from fighting the Taranaki Maori. If they wanted to extend their power they would have to crush the King Movement. So they now turned their attention to the Waikato.

Waikato

I grew up in the Waikato. I was born in Hamilton and spent my childhood years in Cambridge before my parents moved the family to the 'big smoke', Auckland, to search for a better life. Now, like many Aucklanders, I often drive down State Highway 1 to Hamilton and beyond. As I climb the Bombay hills and finally leave Auckland and its endless motorways, my mind starts ticking off the small towns and communities as I go deeper and deeper into the Waikato valley.

Pokeno was always a good place to stop and get an icecream. Mercer had the pub — sadly no longer there; and the power station was at Meremere. At Rangiriri there was another pub, and a decision would be made whether to stop there for a cuppa or continue on to Ohinewai. Then there was Huntly, with the sign outside the brick toilets that read, 'Yes, these are Huntly bricks', reassuring me that I could use the facility without it falling over. On past Taupiri and the sacred hillside; and just down the road from there was Ngaruawahia — a town that fascinates me still with its sense of history and mystery.

Most of these places flash by. If you blink as you go through Rangiriri, you will not notice that you have blasted through what was the site of one of this country's most brutal and bloody battles. There is little to remind a passing traveller that Pokeno was the base camp for the army of Lt-General Cameron; or that Meremere was a huge base of Maori resistance that at times held in excess of 1000 warriors. But the signs are still there.

Mercer is a town with a certain atmosphere. A couple of years ago I went there to photograph it for an assignment. I left Auckland very early in order to get the morning light; but as I rolled over the Bombay hills I was confronted with a fog so thick that I couldn't see the Waikato River, even when I was right beside it. I sat in the car and waited for a while but the fog seemed determined to stay. I got out of the car and walked from State Highway 1 down towards the river. As I did so, I stumbled across the Mercer war memorial. It's a curious affair. The base is a gun turret that came off the Pioneer, *a gunboat under General Cameron's command. Sitting on top of the gun turret is the statue of a World War I soldier.*

The Pioneer *was one of a few gunboats that were used to invade the Waikato in 1863. They were to prove vital. The Great South Road, which had been constructed for the movement of troops and supplies into the Waikato, was under constant attack from the Kingites, to the extent that the invasion by Cameron and his army was stalled by three months. Most of Cameron's forces were deployed in the protection of this road. Once the* Pioneer *arrived, the river could be used as well and the invasion was able to continue.*

The Pioneer *had two turrets: one has ended up at Mercer and the other at Ngaruawahia, where it now sits beside the bandstand on the Ngaruawahia point, where the Waikato and Waipa Rivers meet. At one time the Mercer turret was used by the local police as a temporary lockup — but unsuccessfully, it seems, as whisky could be poured down through the rifle holes to the inmates inside.*

A hill near Mercer, known as Koheroa, was the scene of one of the first major confrontations between the imperial army and the King Movement in the Waikato. On 17 July 1863 Lt-General Cameron and 553 men attacked between 100 and 150 Maori as they

The Pa site at Meremere as it is today.

were completing entrenchments in the hillside. On arriving at the scene Cameron and his men were initially checked by heavy fire coming from the Maori garrison, but Cameron leapt ahead of his men and urged them on. They took the position and forced the Maori back into a ravine, where they escaped and made their way to the main fortifications at Meremere. Estimates of losses among the Maori range from 15 to 30, and the British casualties were 12 men killed or wounded. Lt-General Cameron was recommended for the Victoria Cross as a result of his bravery during this action, but the request was turned down and instead he was reprimanded: generals, he was informed, should never expose themselves to that kind of danger.

Just down the road from Mercer is Meremere. When I was a kid the power station on the banks of the Waikato at Meremere was still operating and the wire cables that transported the coal from some unseen source used to fascinate me. These days the station has been mothballed and sits there like some recently forgotten relic. A road takes you up the hill and into the village which consists of state houses, presumably built for the workers at the station. The houses are

The war memorial at Mercer, whose base is a gun turret from the Pioneer.

of brick (from Huntly?) and the neat gardens that surround them imply that the village is still happily inhabited.

In the centre of the town a small hill rises above the housing. On top of the hill is a water tank covered in graffiti, and a sign indicating that this is a place of historical interest. I figured there had to be something left of what was once a significant fortification, and I wasn't disappointed. The site is well preserved, with the lines of trenches of the British redoubt that was built there after the Maori abandoned the site still plainly visible.

It's not hard to see why this place was so strategic in the defence against the imperial army. The top of the mound provides a view not only of the Waikato River, and anything that might be moving along it, but of the surrounding countryside as well. From here, it's an easy leap of the imagination back to the turbulent years of the 1860s.

Meremere was the central position of the first line of defence for the Kingite Maori in the Waikato. This line extended to Pukekawa in the west and to Paparata in the east. Pukekawa was vital because from there the Waikato River could easily be crossed and raids launched against the supply lines of Cameron's army. The position to the north-east at Paparata protected the right flank at Meremere and also secured the area of land between Thames and Wairoa. Also, much of the supply of guns, ammunition and manpower from the east came up through this region.

Stationed in redoubts at Pokeno, Cameron's forces relied on two lines of supply. The first of these was over the Bombay hills along the newly built Great South Road, and the second was the Waikato River itself. Supplies were loaded at Onehunga and brought by sea to the mouth of the river. They were floated upstream by canoe, then transferred onto gunboats such as the *Avon* and the *Pioneer,* as well as a flotilla of smaller craft. A supply depot was set up at a place on a bend in the river, and was given the name Camerontown for the stockpile of supplies and equipment.

This depot was attacked on 7 September by about 100 Maori based at Pukekawa, and 40 tons of stores and the depot itself were destroyed by fire. Some Maori, loyal to Queen Victoria, who were guarding the depot at the time managed to escape and, finding their way to the redoubt at Tuakau, raised the alarm. A detachment of 50 men set out from Tuakau after the attackers and were met by an ambush. Approaching Camerontown, they heard what they mistakenly thought was a group of drunken Maori. As they charged into action they were met by a terrific volley of musket fire, and were chased back through the bush. Ably led by a Sergeant McKenna, by all accounts they were lucky to escape with only nine casualties.

Ngati Paoa made another attack on a supply convoy midway between Drury and Queens Redoubt at Pokeno. Led by Hori Ngakapa Te Whanaunga, they overpowered the convoy and chased them halfway back to Drury before they were rescued by a detachment of the 18th Regiment. In the course of this action 16 British were killed or wounded, and they also lost several horses and wagons.

PUKEKOHE EAST PRESBYTERIAN CHURCH

On 14 September 1863 this church in Pukekohe was attacked by about 200 Maori of the Ngati Maniapoto tribe in the Waikato. This group had come up from the Meremere line of defence and was joined by a group of Ngati Pou who acted as guides (this had once been Ngati Pou land). The church had been converted into a redoubt and at the time of the attack was manned by only 17 soldiers and special constables, led by Sergeant Perry.

Sergeant Perry's first order was to fix bayonets. He also ordered that on no account were volleys to be fired because if all 17 men were reloading their weapons at once the attackers would have an opportunity to charge. Two of the men, Joseph Scott and James Easton, were considered to be 'crack shots', and they were positioned by a narrow gateway where the Maori had concentrated the thrust of the attack. It was said that they wasted

Pukekohe East Presbyterian Church.

Ngati Maniopoto attack the fortified church. Alexander Turnbull Library F-20011-1/2.

very little ammunition — most of it found its mark. The Maori made various charges and tried to pull the rifles through the loopholes of the stockade, but fortunately for those inside the rifle butts were too big to fit through. The fight that followed was to last most of the day. This tiny defence force was reinforced at about one o'clock by 32 members of the 70th Regiment under Lieutenant Grierson and later on by a detachment of Waikato Militia who brought with them much-needed supplies of ammunition. At about four o'clock 150 men of the 18th Royal Irish and the 65th charged into the clearing in front of the church and engaged the attackers, eventually driving them off.

Amazingly, not one of the original defenders of the church was hit by gunfire, though the British lost three men and eight were wounded. In this engagement 40 Maori lost their lives.

There is a story attached to this event. Apparently a kereru (wood pigeon), dazed and confused by the noise and smoke of the battle, flew up onto the roof of the church and stayed there for most of the day without being harmed. The defenders of the church took this to be a good omen.

Lt-General Cameron, who was coming under increasing pressure from the government and the press to continue the invasion of the Waikato, must have wondered what he had let himself in for. The raids mentioned above were only two of many, and close to 80 per cent of his army was now occupied in ferrying commissariat stores and guarding the supply lines from Kingite attack.

With the arrival of the *Pioneer* and an extra 500 men, Cameron was ready to advance on Meremere. The entrenchments at Meremere were extensive and the number of warriors stationed there fluctuated, probably between 1000 and 2000. In addition they had three cannon which they were using to cover any attack made by gunboat from the river. These guns had been manhandled over the ranges from Kawhia to the Waipa River, then taken by canoe down the Waipa and Waikato Rivers to Meremere. The crews who fired these weapons were trained well enough, but a shortage of proper ammunition limited their effectiveness considerably.

On 29 and 30 October the *Pioneer* with Cameron on board reconnoitred the Kingite entrenchments. Anchoring about 300 yards from shore they remained there for a couple of hours under fire from the Maori garrison. The cannon at Meremere opened up, firing anything from canisters of nails to lengths of chain, to little effect. At one point a seven pound weight was fired over to the *Pioneer* and managed to pierce its side. Unfortunately for the Meremere defenders, this weight lodged itself in a casket of beef on board and failed to do any further damage.

With the reconnaissance completed Cameron transported 600 men on the *Pioneer*

THE WAR IN NEW ZEALAND: THE GUN-BOAT PIONEER AT ANCHOR OFF MEREMERE, ON THE WAIKATO RIVER, RECONNOITRING THE NATIVE POSITION.

Engraving of the gunboat Pioneer *at anchor off Meremere, October, 1863.*

Alexander Turnbull Library F-112772-1/2.

and the *Avon* as well as some smaller craft to a position some eight miles to the rear of Meremere. There artillery was put in place and a gunboat was left at anchor in the river to cut off that avenue of escape. The rest of the gunboats then returned to pick up a further 600 men who were to be deployed in such a way as to cut off retreat from the rear and the left flank. The Meremere garrison, realising the danger, launched an attack against the gun emplacements, but this was repulsed. Before the second 600 soldiers were in place for the attack, the Kingites abandoned Meremere via the flooded swamp at the rear. The Maori seldom built a fortified position that did not allow for evacuation, and the high water in the swamp enabled them to escape by canoe without any loss of life.

Cameron's intention was to block any possible escape route and then launch an attack that would finish the King Movement. Instead he had to content himself with building a redoubt on the Meremere site and moving his army to the next line of defence, at Rangiriri.

RANGIRIRI

A small section of the trenches remains at Rangiriri. On the right-hand side of State Highway 1 just as you enter Rangiriri from the north is a carefully tended and fenced portion of what was once the central redoubt of a defence line that started on the bank of the Waikato and stretched right across to Lake Waikare on the left. There is a very quiet atmosphere here. This place, on 20 November 1863, was the scene of one of the most desperate battles ever to occur during the New Zealand Wars, and it's as if the immediate quiet that follows the roar of guns still lingers.

Across the road is a cemetery that contains the remains of many who fell during the battle of Rangiriri. Here Maori and British soldiers share their final resting-place — the Maori on their home ground and the English and Irish so far away from theirs.

The tearooms of Rangiriri are worth dropping in to for a cuppa. The muffins are always fresh and the place itself has been converted into a mini-museum with artefacts from the battle. The owners know the history of the area well, and were very patient with me and my endless stream of questions.

On 20 November 1863 General Cameron and about 1300 men and officers made an assault on Maori fortifications at Rangiriri. These fortifications consisted of a series of

The Rangiriri Hotel, which is an important local landmark today.

trenches and parapets that spanned a line from Lake Waikare to the Waikato River. At the centre of this line was the main redoubt. The earthworks were protected from the front by a series of ditches which, from the bottom to the top of the parapet, measured some 21 feet and gave the attacking party approximately 9 feet to bridge. To the rear of this position, entrenched lines of rifle pits were constructed that ran parallel to the Waikato River, to obstruct any advance made from that direction.

Cameron's strategy was to attack the Maori position from the front and rear. He realised that although the fortifications were considerable, the 400–500 Maori entrenched there would not be enough to defend a prolonged attack from both sides at once. Also, he wanted a decisive victory — he did not want the defenders to escape, as had happened at Meremere two weeks previously.

Having placed 770 of his force to the north of the position, he organised a further 500 to the rear by way of the *Pioneer* and the *Avon*. As these boats (towing two gunboats) had difficulty negotiating the currents of the Waikato River, the troops on board were late in making landfall and getting themselves into position; but in spite of this General Cameron ordered bombardment to commence at three o'clock with the two Armstrong guns in his complement.

The graveyard at Rangiriri with the graves of those who fell during the battle.

A photograph of the earthworks at Rangiriri taken shortly after the battle. Hawke's Bay Museum.

The bombardment had little effect against the earthworks, so at 4.30 pm Cameron ordered a series of assaults, the first of which was carried out by the 65th Regiment. After bitter fighting the 65th had succeeded in forcing the Maori from the weaker points in the line and into the central redoubt; then they in turn were forced to retreat. Three more assaults were made — one, curiously, by only 36 members of the Royal Artillery led by Captain Mercer, who was mortally wounded during the charge, having been shot through the mouth; and two by 90 of the Naval Brigade, led by Commander Mayne of HMS *Eclipse*. The Maori position was too strong for the British troops, however, and as night fell they were deployed around it to stop any escape and a trench was started with the intention of sapping and blowing up the parapet.

During the course of the night, however, some of the Maori did escape, and the following morning a white flag appeared over the parapet. The British took the opportunity and marched into the redoubt and took control. After the battle of Rangiriri, 36 Maori dead were found and 183 were taken prisoner; and 41 British were dead. The Waikato region was now open for General Cameron.

For a long time it was believed that the Maori garrison at Rangiriri surrendered to the British because they were surrounded and had ammunition supply problems. But it has since been established that many Maori had escaped the fortifications, including Wiremu Tamehana and also possibly King Tawhiao. It would have been a disaster for the King

Movement if these individuals had been taken prisoner. Also it has been established that many of the wounded had left the position during the night.

So it would appear that 'being surrounded' wasn't the problem. It also seems unlikely that the Maori garrison would run out of ammunition, as there were reports of a good supply on hand when the 'surrender' occurred. Many of the prisoners taken at Rangiriri expressed surprise at having been overrun by the British, as the raising of the white flag was meant to show only a wish to negotiate. Up to this point the battle had gone well for the Maori, who had demonstrated that they could withstand all the assaults thrown at them, so it seems possible that they intended to negotiate from what they would have seen as a strong position.

The prisoners were shipped to Auckland, where they were kept in prison hulks in conditions that could only be described as inhumane. Eventually they were incarcerated on Kawau Island, and all escaped 10 months later. The way they were treated, however, was thought to be one of the reasons Maori were reluctant to surrender in future battles.

NGARUAWAHIA

The centre of the Maori King Movement, Ngaruawahia, was next on the list. General Cameron's forces marched into this town and took it unopposed. King Tawhiao had since retreated into Ngati Maniapoto territory further south in the Waikato, where he was to remain for the next 18 years. This new area became known as the 'King Country'.

Ngaruawahia was, and still is, the seat of Maori sovereignty. The King Movement was established not as a threat to the sovereignty of Queen Victoria, as the settlers at the time believed, but as a way of controlling the sale of Maori land and protecting the Maori way of life. Wiremu Tamehana had travelled to Auckland just after the movement was established, in order to talk to the colonial authorities of its intentions and to suggest some form of Maori involvement in colonial government. At Auckland he was kept waiting while storekeepers and others were granted an audience. There was only so much of this humiliation he could take, and he returned to the Waikato without being heard. A golden opportunity was lost.

The British army marched into Ngaruawahia unopposed. The house of the Maori king was occupied and the British flag now flew from its flagstaff. By the time Cameron got there, however, he was starting to have doubts about the war he was embroiled in. Certainly there was no evidence of any Kingite invasion of Auckland, which many believed had been a genuine threat, and the opportunity of a decisive victory over the King Movement had failed, once at Meremere and again at Rangiriri. Cameron was also

Ngaruawahia Point.

From inside the Pioneer *gun turret on Ngaruawahia Point.*

well aware that the unacceptable loss of life during the bitter fighting at Rangiriri had yielded little in terms of strategic value. The Kingite army had merely moved to another line of defence based at Paterangi, and these defences were virtually unassailable, as Cameron was to discover.

At Ngaruawahia, however, Wiremu Tamehana and other 'moderate' leaders of the Kingites showed a willingness to negotiate a peaceful settlement. Cameron was also ready for peace and messages were quickly sent to Governor Grey. Grey, however, came under pressure from the Whitaker administration not to accept. Frederick Whitaker and his business partner, Thomas Russell, were owners of the Bank of New Zealand — a bank that handled many of the loans used to buy land — and were both involved in a land speculation company set up with Donald McLean, who acted as government land purchasing agent as well as eventually becoming the native affairs minister.

It was Whitaker who gave New Zealand the Native Settlement Act, by which the governor could, on the advice of his ministers (ie Whitaker and Russell), confiscate the land of Maori rebels, and that land could be used to establish settlements for immigrant farmers. It is worth noting that the land confiscated was not that of individual rebels but

King Matutaera's whare, Ngaruawahia, photographed in 1864.

of whole districts. In effect the government could take whatever land it wanted. Also, Whitaker had made provision for a huge loan of three million pounds (to be handled by the Bank of New Zealand) on the London market and it was assumed that this money would be repaid by the sale of land. Furthermore, 5000 military settlers had been recruited, many before the war began, and part of the deal for these men was a land grant — land that had yet to be found. Thus it is not surprising that the Whitaker administration was reluctant to talk peace. Whitaker and Russell needed as many 'rebels' as they could find, or create. However, it would be unwise and perhaps unfair to suggest that Whitaker and co were solely responsible for the outbreak of war in the Waikato — they were certainly not the only ones to use to personal advantage an attitude that existed among the immigrant settlers of the time.

For the Kingites, surrender would have meant the loss of all land except that set aside by the government as reserves; and the laying down of all arms. A surrender of this nature was not what the Maori had in mind, so the war continued. Cameron advanced further into the Waikato via the Waipa River, and Tamehana built a pa at Maungatautari and stated, 'If the Governor follows me here, I shall fight. If not I shall remain quiet . . . But if the General goes to Waipa (to attack) the Ngati Maniapoto I shall be there.'

I was driving around the Pirongia area trying to find something of the Paterangi defences that have now been well and truly ploughed under, and found Waiare Road. A battle referred to as the 'Waiare incident' came to mind and this road seemed a likely place. Waiare Road comes to a dead end and a noise from under my car bonnet suggested that I was about to as well. I lifted the bonnet and to the delight of my male ego found the problem: a bolt had come loose and the alternator was threatening to commit suicide by throwing itself onto the road.

I had my head buried in the engine trying to sort all this out when a passing farmer stopped and offered assistance. I told him who I was and what I was doing in his neck of the woods, and asked if he knew anything about it. He pointed out the hill on a neighbouring property that was once the Paterangi defence line, and it was plain that there was nothing left of it. He also said that part of the defences extended onto his farm. He pointed out an area that had been used as a hospital of sorts, and said I was welcome to check it out. I wandered off across his land, and after sorting out which fences were electric and which were not — no mean feat for a city boy — I found the spot. It certainly had the right feel, and I was soon standing on what appeared to be the remnants of old earthworks with trench lines still visible. The light was fading rapidly and a mist was coming in from Mount Pirongia. The place where I was standing was covered with old trees, their limbs all tortured and twisted. It was magic.

Waiare/Paterangi.

PATERANGI

After the fall of Meremere the Maori garrison fell back to Paterangi and there started the most extensive series of defensive pa and entrenchments in the whole of the war. The base of this line was Paterangi itself. The fortifications here consisted mainly of trenches and bombproof bunkers that were concentrated in three main redoubts. This massive structure was, however, only one of four main pa designed to protect the fertile Rangiaowhia district and to halt the advance of the imperial army. Rangiaowhia was one of the principal food-growing areas of the Waikato, and before the war it had sold much of its produce to the Auckland and Sydney markets. Now it was the main source of food for the Waikato Maori and its loss would be a much greater blow for the Kingites than any land so far conceded.

The other three main pa were Pikopiko, Rangiatea, and Manga-pukatea. All were within five or six miles of each other and were capable of assisting each other in the event of an attack. They were positioned in such a way as to block the imperial army's advance on Rangiaowhia from any of the main routes. Estimates of the numbers garrisoned there range from 1000 to 3000, and certainly around 2000 would have been needed to complete the fortifications in time for Cameron's arrival.

Lt-General Cameron meanwhile had a few problems of his own. As the supply line became longer, the difficulties in protecting it became greater. By January Cameron had 7000 men in the Ngaruawahia area: half of these were dedicated to securing his supplies and communications. Also, on 8 February the *Avon* sank in the Waipa River after hitting a submerged tree. This boat was capable of carrying 25–30 tons of equipment on each trip as well as towing various smaller craft, and its loss was a disaster. A third steamer, the *Koheroa*, had just arrived in Auckland and was still just a shell, but it was decided to launch her and send her down to Cameron with 30 tons of supplies. After an eventful voyage in which she burst several plates at the Waikato Heads and threatened to sink, the *Koheroa* arrived at Te Rore where the main camp had been set up, and the invasion was able to restart.

Te Rore was a couple of miles from Paterangi and Lt-General Cameron had an advance camp set up there, under the command of Colonel Waddy. Cameron correctly assumed that an assault against the Kingite entrenchments would be far too expensive in terms of lives, so no attack was made. Instead, the garrisons on both side busied themselves with long-range sniping, occasional shelling from the British, and the odd skirmish or two. The only major action occurred at a place called Waiare.

Through Waiare runs the Mangapiko Stream, and at a point about a mile south of Paterangi the stream forms a loop, encompassing about 18 acres of land. At the neck of

Earthworks at Paterangi, February 1864. Hawke's Bay Museum.

the loop were some disused Maori fortifications, consisting of three large parapets with trenches that ran across the neck at right angles to the stream. A Maori raiding party were in hiding amongst the parapets and preparing themselves for a night raid on Colonel Waddy's advance camp. While they waited, a lightly armed group of soldiers from the 40th Regiment came down to the stream for a swim. Unable to resist the temptation the Maori opened fire, and before long all hell broke loose. The firing was heard from the advance camp and the bathers were quickly reinforced by members of the 40th and 50th Regiments as well as Captain Jackson of the Forest Rangers and Charles Heaphy of the Auckland Rifle Volunteers. Jackson sent word back to the main camp at Te Rore, and was soon joined by Captain von Tempsky and a group of Forest Rangers. The British and colonial troops gathered on the outside of the stream's loop and began to skirmish their way towards the Maori position. What followed was intense fighting at very close quarters that left the Maori with 40 dead and 30 wounded, and the British 6 dead and 5 wounded. Captain Charles Heaphy (who was a staff surveyor) was awarded the Victoria Cross for the bravery he showed during this action. He was the first irregular in the British empire to receive the medal and the only colonial soldier in the New Zealand Wars to do so.

RANGIAOWHIA

A friend of mine, John Buddle, who is a Vietnam veteran, told me that in the heat of battle when mates are getting hurt or killed, tension and tempers run high. In these circumstances, surrendering to the enemy is a tricky business and the risk of being shot on sight is real. Such was the case at Rangiaowhia in 1864, where some Kingite defenders came out of a house after being surrounded and were shot by over-enthusiastic soldiers of the imperial and colonial army. There was confusion over this incident, with both officers and men trying to restore order. This unfortunate and unnecessary episode has left scars that have proved slow to heal.

Prior to the war Rangiaowhia was an area of intense cultivation. Hundreds of acres were planted with potatoes, wheat, and maize for the Auckland market and the land was considered to be the very best. It was a source of envy for settlers wanting more land. Another bone of contention for them was the fact that much of this land was farmed collectively. This made it hard for settlers to compete.

Today the area is still farmland and appears to be as productive as ever, though the only building to survive the 1860s is the Anglican church on Rangiaowhia Road. This building was a place of refuge for many Maori when Cameron's troops attacked on 21 February 1864.

RANGIAOWHIA AND HAIRINI

With the losses suffered at Rangiriri still fresh in his mind, the decision not to launch any frontal assault on the defences at Paterangi was not a difficult one for Cameron — Paterangi was far more sophisticated than Rangiriri and also a good deal larger. Instead, he planned to outflank this position by bypassing it and taking Rangiaowhia. Rangiaowhia was crucial to the Waikato Maori. It supplied the Maori garrison with all its food, and was also the centre of the Waikato's economic wealth. Cameron figured that, if this place were taken, the Paterangi line might fall without the need for any assault; or, better still, the garrison there would rush to protect it, thus forcing them out into the open. If this could be done Cameron felt sure of a decisive victory over the Kingites, as fighting on open ground was something the British army was very good at.

Cameron's first problem was to move 1200 men past the Paterangi fortifications and on to Rangiaowhia without detection. A part-Maori by the name of James Edward, or Himi Manuao, who had lived in Rangiaowhia before the war, had agreed to act as a guide, and on the night of 20 February 1864 Cameron and members of the 65th, 70th and 50th Regiments, along with No. 2 Company of the Forest Rangers under von Tempsky, the

Soldiers of the Light Company 65th (Yorkshire North Riding) Regiment.
Alexander Turnbull Library F-25608-1/2.

Colonial Defence Force Cavalry under Colonel Nixon and the Mounted Artillery under Lieutenant Rait, set off. No. 1 Company of the Forest Rangers made up the rear guard. A sufficient force was left behind at the advance camp, whose task it was to notify Cameron should he and his column be detected. The moonless night was perfect for the march and as they had to pass within 1500 yards of the Paterangi position, the men were told to carry with them as little as possible, and that the strictest silence had to be observed. They passed Paterangi close enough to hear the call of the Kingite sentries, and that they were not noticed is a remarkable achievement — British regulars were not famous for their ability to march in silence. The troops marched through the night, and as dawn came they passed the village of Te Awamutu and carried on to Rangiaowhia, three miles distant.

As they approached their destination, Colonel Nixon's cavalry moved ahead of the main column, and shooting was soon to be heard. There were about 100 men in the settlement, and as many women and children. Many of the occupants fled as the main force came up and began skirmishing from building to building. Von Tempsky and his rangers came to the Catholic church where some of the villagers had made a stand. The villagers were soon surrounded, and when a white flag was shown from the window, von Tempsky was ordered to leave them alone. He did so reluctantly.

The main fighting was now centred on a whare containing 10 warriors who were putting up a determined resistance. What happened next is described in the following account, almost certainly written by Captain Wilson of the Colonial Defence Force Cavalry who fought at the battle.

It carries me back to the Sunday morning (21 February 1864) when our Colonel Nixon fell mortally wounded, and two of our corporals were killed, McHale inside the whare and Alexander at the door. Corporal Dunn too received a bullet, which, I believe, he still carries in his body; also two of the 65th Regiment were wounded, one mortally, and one of the Forest Rangers. The night before we paraded at 11 o'clock at Te Rore, and then moved off quietly. We knew something was up. We were to get round the enemy and take him in the rear, or something like that. The way was led by von Tempsky's Forest Rangers, followed by the 65th and 70th Regiments, the Naval Brigade, the Mounted Artillery, and the Defence Force, while Jackson's company of Rangers brought up the rear. The night was dark and we groped our way along a Maori track, passing pretty close to the Maori position at Pikopiko. At cock-crow we entered Te Awamutu. The bridge had been broken up but the planks were there, and to relay was the work of but a few minutes. This done, the order was given, 'Forward the Cavalry', and away we went, the Defence Force and Rait's Mounted Artillerymen. It did not take long to clear the enemy out of Rangiaowhia, our infantry being far in the rear. Having accomplished our work, we turned about, and were taking prisoners as we came along, when my attention was drawn to the whare shewn in the picture by a struggle going on close to it, between Corporal Little of ours, and a huge Maori. Little having secured his man, I ordered Corporal McHale to make prisoners of the Maori, who we could hear talking inside. Six men and a youth were seen to enter the whare. McHale entered the hut, but no sooner

British troops at Rangiaowhia, February 1864. Hawke's Bay Museum

St Paul's Anglican Church, Rangiaowhia.

had he passed the door than I heard two shots fired, apparently from the Corporal's revolver. I called out 'What the —— are you shooting at the Maori for?', jumped from my horse and was into the hut in a moment. The doorway was very low, you had to stoop low on entering. The place was full of smoke, and as I entered under me lay McHale's body, his feet towards the door, and face down. I could see nobody else in the darkness and smoke. I backed out, calling out that McHale had been shot; and now with our carbines we commenced to riddle the house which was built of slabs. The firing soon brought together the whole of the Cavalry; and after a while some of the 65th and the Forest Rangers. Also the General and staff, came up. After General Cameron's arrival Colonel Nixon was shot from the door of the whare as shewn in the picture. Then, as the Maori did not surrender when challenged again, the infantry fired the house. I saw one Maori walk out of the blazing hut, his blanket singed in his back. Poor fellow! he fell within ten paces of the door whence he and his compatriots had so wantonly shot our Colonel and many good men. There was nothing now to prevent us from recovering McHale's body, and, such as it was, hard to distinguish from the Maori around him, we bore it away.

The sun was overhead and baking hot as we moved slowly with our dead and wounded back to Te Awamutu. The wounded suffered much from fatigue and heat, and the enemy followed us up and fired at us along the way. I mention that in the pursuit, before the whare was attacked, the Maori, men and women, were jumbled together, running away, and, being dressed much alike, the women were in great danger of being killed, and as I had command of the advance guard, I called out to the women, telling them to sit down, 'E kotou, e nga wahine e noho ki raro, kei mate kotou.' They obeyed, and we passed them; they then got up and ran on.

I heard some days afterward that the big Maori whom I mentioned before as having been taken prisoner had said that his life was saved by a man who wore a silver band around his cap. I write this simply to shew that we did try to save the natives.

It was a sad day, of course, for all concerned; but as they have asserted we kohuru (murdered) them, I have endeavoured to shew how they brought about their own destruction by wantonly killing our men at a time when they were surrounded and had no chance of escape.

At the great Maori meeting at Kopua, twelve months ago last May, I met two gentlemen, Wesleyan ministers, who informed me that there was but one thing the natives were sore about, namely, the kohuru at Rangiaowhia. I replied 'I can explain about that affair, for I was present. It was I who sent the man whom the Maori shot into the hut to make prisoners. Our man was dead inside the hut before the attack commenced.' And I offered to meet the natives and tell them how it had all happened.

After the action at Hairini, I made a rough sketch of the ground where Colonel Nixon had fallen, showing the positions of several huts there, and how the combatants were placed, and the picture of the fight at Rangiaowhia is based on this sketch.

Our old Colonel's revolver lies under the table where I write, but he slumbers in the cemetery at Auckland, awaiting the great reveille, when they who fell in that hut will bear witness to the truth of this defence of the Defence Force.

THE FIGHT AT RANGIAOHIA FOR THE RECOVERY OF McHALE'S BODY.
FEBRUARY 21, 1864.

A lithograph of the gun battle at Rangiaowhia. Alexander Turnbull Library F-38105-1/2.

As Captain Wilson mentions, the actions at Rangiaowhia were the cause of considerable ill feeling on the part of the Maori. Their discontent was over the unnecessary shooting of men who should have been taken as prisoners of war. No inquiry was held into the conduct of the troops, probably as a result of a clause in the Suppression of Rebellion Act 1863 that indemnified all those who committed questionable acts while in the course of suppressing rebellion.

After securing Rangiaowhia, Cameron withdrew his troops to Te Awamutu and waited there for reinforcements to be brought up and also to see how the Kingite forces at Paterangi would react. The next day it was reported to Cameron that the Kingites had reoccupied Rangiaowhia and had thrown up defences on Hairini Ridge, situated between Rangiaowhia and Cameron's forces at Te Awamutu. Cameron decided to attack Hairini before the entrenchments there were completed.

The battle that followed was an anticlimax. It seems that Wiremu Tamehana intended to delay Cameron as long as possible in order for the bulk of his force to escape and carry with them as much as they could out of Rangiaowhia. The force that Cameron's men faced at Hairini was light — about 400 — and these men quickly fell back after the first assaults of the imperial army. Tamehana stated that the Kingites lost nine men in this action. The British casualties were three killed and 15 wounded.

You can see the movie Rewi's Last Stand *on request at the Te Awamutu Museum. It's a slice of New Zealand history, and good fun to watch as well. Some of the historical material is accurate; and the movie helped to make the battle of Orakau perhaps the most famous of all the events that took place during these wars. Also at the Te Awamutu Museum is a 12-pounder Armstrong gun that was used not only in the movie but apparently at the battle itself — and it's still in remarkably good condition.*

The site of the battle is not much to look at these days. The monument was erected in 1914 and, according to historian Christopher Pugsley, the map of the site on the nearby plaque is upside down. So if you're like me and go to the place and can't figure it all out, this might explain why. Anyway, that's my excuse and I'm sticking to it.

The battle must have been a desperate time for the defenders of the pa. They had no food or water, were firing peachstones instead of proper ammunition, and with the sap of the imperial and colonial forces getting nearer and nearer, the whole experience must have been hell. My

Memorial plaque to fallen Maori, inside St John's Church, Te Awamutu.

father told me that when he was a boy of about 10 he used to visit an old man whom he knew as Paki. Paki told my father that when he was a boy of about two or three years of age he was at the battle of Orakau. His memory of the event was sketchy, but it must have made a big impression for an old man in his seventies to remember something that happened so long ago. He said that he remembers holding his mother's hand and being told to run. His mother was holding another infant in her arms. The only other thing he remembers was his father's face being covered in blood.

ORAKAU

After the fall of Rangiaowhia, the British forces were either concentrating on Tamehana's pa at Maungatautari or guarding the land already confiscated. This gave the Kingite Maori a lull in which they could consider their options, and a meeting was called between the Ngati Maniapoto and their allies at a village called Wharepapa, just south of the Puniu River. Rewi Maniapoto wanted a further meeting with Wiremu Tamehana before any final decision was made, and was on his way to see him when he came across a group of Tuhoe and Ngati Ruakawa warriors. These men had formed part of the defences at Paterangi and, under the leadership of a group of chiefs including Piripi Te Heuheu and Te Whenua-nui, had come a long way to fight the Pakeha. As such they were reluctant to go back to their home in the Urewera without a confrontation. They pressured Rewi to allow them to make a stand at Orakau. Orakau was the favoured position as it was right under the noses of the British and, if a pa were constructed there, Cameron's forces at Te Awamutu and Kihikihi would be obliged to attack.

Rewi was opposed to the plan. Orakau was Ngati Maniapoto land and Rewi did not want to risk any unnecessary action that might result in its confiscation. Also, he objected to the site they had chosen on which to make this stand — and with good reason. The site was flawed in several ways. First, it was on ground that by traditional standards was too low to defend easily; second, it had no water supply; and third, the position was one that could be completely surrounded, with no provision for an evacuation route. But Rewi was in an awkward political position — it was he who had asked these men to come and fight in the first place. Also, among them were some of his kinfolk. Whatever his objections, the stand was made at Orakau and it was Rewi who led it.

One of the advantages of the site was that it could be constructed quickly. Working in relay teams as there were not enough shovels and other implements to go around, the Maori constructed a fortification that measured 80 feet by 40 feet. It consisted of a trench and a broad parapet about six feet thick. The parapet was made of alternating layers of earth and fern, giving it an elastic quality that could absorb the shock of shell fire. Inside

The Orakau monument with the upside down map of the battle site at its base.

the pa were earthworks designed to protect the inhabitants as much as possible from shelling, and surrounding the whole affair was a pekerangi that acted much as barbed wire did in later wars. The defending garrison consisted of no more than 300, representing many different tribes from all over the North Island, though the bulk of this force were Tuhoe and Ngati Ruakawa. Included in this number were many women and some children.

On 30 March 1864 the work was still being completed at Orakau. Two surveyors, Mr Gundry and Mr Wilson, were working on a hillside at Kihikihi and spotted the garrison through their theodolite. They quickly relayed the news to Brigadier-General G. J. Carey. Although Lt-General Cameron and 1000 men were facing Tamehana's pa at Maungatautari, Carey was able to put together a force of about 1100 men and with these he proceeded immediately to Orakau, where they arrived on the morning of 31 March.

It would seem that Carey's first intention was to surround the pa site, but this position appeared to be a weak one, so an assault led by Captain Ring was immediately launched. This took the Kingites by surprise, but with a carefully organised series of volleys orchestrated by Rewi, the attack was easily repulsed. It was followed by another assault, also led by Captain Ring, with the same result, and among the casualties was Ring himself. A third assault led by Captain Baker was also to prove useless and Carey, having got the message that the place was stronger than it first appeared, had the pa surrounded. In doing so he cut off the water supply and exposed the pa's greatest weakness; but for the moment at least, the morale of the Kingites inside was high.

Up to this point there had been no decisive victory in the Waikato campaign. Cameron had wanted a battle that would crush the Kingites and the King Movement once and for all, and Carey now saw an opportunity for this to happen. He sent word to Cameron of the events that had occurred and Cameron responded at once. He sent reinforcements, which arrived on 1 April, and he joined Carey in the field the following day.

In the meantime, however, the battle raged. Carey had moved his troops as close as possible to the Maori defences, where they dug trenches of their own and began firing. The return fire of the Kingites had forced the troops back on a number of occasions, and soon after encircling the pa, Carey ordered that a flying sap be dug towards the Maori position. It was thought that the sap would reach the Maori position by midnight, but attacks against it held up completion for another 36 hours. Artillery was used, but due to the strength of the entrenchment it had little effect.

By the end of the first day, however, the Maori were having problems of their own. The water supply was fast running out, as was the ammunition, in spite of the care with which it was being used. Orakau was built in the midst of a grove of peach trees, and as the siege continued, peachstones were being used instead of lead bullets.

By the third day the sap had reached very close to the Maori entrenchments and Cameron, who had arrived earlier that day, offered Rewi a chance to surrender. Rewi refused, saying, 'My friend, I will fight you for ever, for ever.' It was then suggested that the women and children be allowed to leave, and the response was, 'If the men die, the women and children will also die.' But by the afternoon the situation was hopeless and the Maori garrison did something that was never expected — they evacuated.

This action took Cameron's troops completely by surprise. Rewi and his followers, with the women and children in the centre and the warriors surrounding them, left the pa and moved off in a controlled fashion. They approached the 40th Regiment who were holding their part of the line, and before Cameron and his men could properly react, had broken through. At this point they split into smaller groups and made for some cover offered by an area of teatree and swamp. The Forest Rangers and Colonial Defence Force Cavalry with some Royal Artillery troopers gave chase — and the battle of Orakau entered its last and less than honourable phase. These forces hunted down what Maori they could and most of the Maori killed in this battle died during this action.

The British losses at Orakau were 16 killed and 53 wounded, some mortally. There is confusion over the exact number of Maori casualties. Rewi stated that 80 died, and it seems reasonable to accept this as accurate although other estimates have been almost twice this number. Much has been said of the courage of the Kingites at Orakau and certainly the British troops that fought them were full of admiration for them, as they were also at Rangiriri. At St John's Church at Te Awamutu is a plaque from the 65th Regiment dedicated to the Maori who fought and died at Rangiaowhia and Orakau. The British and colonial troops often expressed admiration for their Maori enemies once they had been defeated, but were less than gracious if the Maori had won. The plaque at the church though suggests that the sentiments expressed were genuine.

During the Waikato campaign, over 1.2 million acres of land had been confiscated, some 300,000 acres of which was eventually returned. Settlements such as Hamilton, Pirongia and Cambridge soon sprang up on the confiscated land. Many of the settlers were soldiers, and part of the deal offered to colonial soldiers involved land grants: the amount offered depended on the soldier's rank. It was felt that this added to the security of the communities. Often, however, the land granted to soldiers was of poor quality, and much of it was sold to land speculators at the first opportunity.

The land courts, set up as a result of the Native Land Acts of 1862 and 1865 were a far more brutal and efficient way of removing land from Maori ownership. Over a thirty-year period 4 million hectares (approximately 10,000,000 acres) had changed hands as a direct result of these courts. With the loss of the land the identity of the Maori people

An artists' impression of the taking of the pa at Orakau, published in the Illustrated London News, *July 30, 1864.* Alexander Turnbull Library G-21113-1/2.

came under threat. Tribes, subtribes and even individual members of the same family were to start fighting amongst themselves over land titles, and with the loss of land came the loss also of an economic base that would have held the tribe together.

Another government initiative was that of breaking up tribal land into individual titles, and land courts were set up for this purpose. Many Maori were under pressure to secure titles to land they felt was theirs, before someone else did — more often than not a title would be granted to the first person who applied for it, irrespective of who actually owned the land, so if you didn't turn up and defend your claim you might lose out. Of course, once a land title had been secured it was easily sold. Hearings for titles could drag on for weeks, even months, and stories abound of land speculators offering financial support to claimants while the hearings proceeded.

Defending a claim was an expensive business: claimants were away from home and had to feed and house themselves. They were also encouraged to have legal representation. Once a title was granted, the successful claimant was then given a bill covering all costs, often at inflated prices; and frequently the only way for this to be paid was through the sale of the land that had just been secured.

There was an attitude among the European settlers that 'civilisation' had to be instilled into the native population. It was this civilisation that was also used to take everything they had away from them, both legally and through the use of military might.

GATE PA

These days battles are still being fought out on the Gate Pa battle site, but instead of muskets and cannons the combatants use tennis balls and bowls. A bowling green and tennis courts now occupy the land where a battle was once fought which became one of the more embarrassing episodes of British army history. Across the road from the courts is the Gate Pa monument, resting on a rise surrounded by a very pretty park. It was towards the end of spring when I visited Tauranga and the day was hot with a clear blue sky. I had the place to myself apart from several pairs of lovers sprawled about on the grass. They would occasionally look up from their activities and glance suspiciously in my direction as I hovered, camera in hand. I felt like I was a trenchcoat away from being arrested.

The timing of Lt-General Duncan Cameron's return to Auckland coincided with the arrival of news from Brigadier-General Carey regarding a build-up of activity at Tauranga. The situation in Tauranga differed from the Waikato War in that it was not an exercise in the conquest of territory; instead, it was an effort to stop the flow of support for Waikato tribes from Ngai Te Rangi Maori at Tauranga. Ngai Te Rangi had declared themselves to be neutral, and Carey, who was soon to be replaced by Colonel Greer, had been sent by Governor Grey with a small expeditionary force to control the harbour and assess the situation, without attacking any forces that might be genuinely neutral.

The Ngai Te Rangi, however, had begun to make aggressive movements. Under their war chief, Rawiri Puhirake, they built a pa three miles from Te Papa where the British had their camp. The pa was called Pukehinahina, though it is now more commonly known as Gate Pa. When the pa was near completion, Rawiri sent a challenge to Greer to come and fight, and this challenge was soon followed up with an offer to build a road for Greer's forces from Te Papa to the Pukehinahina Pa. Rawiri's strategy was in line with what was becoming the most effective way of fighting the British, that is, to choose the time and place for the confrontation, and also to avoid fighting on open ground. What Rawiri probably hadn't reckoned on was the arrival of Cameron from Auckland with 1700 troops and the biggest artillery train ever to be used in the whole of the New Zealand Wars.

For Cameron the positioning of Pukehinahina was an opportunity to achieve the decisive victory that had so far eluded him. The pa site was on the harbour, which meant he could move as many men and as much equipment as he liked without the supply problems of the Waikato campaign. He wasted no time and arrived at Tauranga on 21 April 1864, with the bulk of his force following him there five days later.

The task must have appeared straightforward to Cameron. On 28 April he sent Greer

The monument at the Pukehinahina Pa site (Gate Pa).

with 730 men of the 68th Regiment to the rear of the pa to cut off any retreat. To get around the pa Greer had to cover nearly a mile of tidal mud flats and would have been exposed to fire from the 230 warriors under Rawiri's command. Cameron ordered a feigned attack on the front of the pa as a diversion, and Greer was able to carry out the manœuvre successfully. On 29 April the bombardment — the heaviest in the whole of the wars — commenced, and it continued throughout that day and the next. In spite of the fact that the Maori had erected a false target in the form of a flag and possibly some fortifications 60 yards behind the main position, and that some gunners had fallen for this ruse, in general the bombardment was a success. The bombardment produced a breach in the Maori defences, and an assault party of 300 men from the 43rd Regiment under Colonel Booth and the Naval Brigade under Commander Hay stormed the pa. These men were supported by another contingent of the Naval Brigade and 43rd, and 180 men under Major Ryan — in all about 800 men. The storming party gained entrance to the pa easily enough, but within 10 minutes came pouring out again in total confusion. It was a complete rout.

Normally troops would expect the greatest resistance as they approached a pa, but at Pukehinahina, instead of manning the outer trenches, the occupants waited in the bomb-proof shelters until the assault party had entered before opening fire. The inside of the pa was a complex arrangement of trenches and bunkers, and when the 43rd and the Naval Brigade entered it must have seemed that the ground beneath them had erupted with a series of lethal volleys. In effect the pa itself was a trap. In the fighting that followed some of the Maori garrison retreated, only to be forced back inside by the firing of the 68th in the rear. The volleys from the 68th probably added to the confusion, by leading the troops to believe that Maori reinforcements had arrived, and within minutes the assault party retreated, leaving behind many dead and wounded. Cameron was furious. Afterwards he apparently refused to visit the wounded officers in his command — an action that was out of character. In the days that followed everybody blamed everybody else for what could only be described as a total disaster. What few people did was give credit to the genius of Rawiri Puhirake.

Arawa Victory over the East Coast Tribes

During the course of the New Zealand Wars many Maori sided with the Pakeha imperial and colonial forces. Their reasons for doing so were varied. The Wanganui Maori, for example, had originally sold the land on which the township was built, and profited greatly from the commerce it generated. Therefore, when the town came under threat it was to their advantage to defend it. This they did on more than one occasion. In May 1864 the tribes from the upper Wanganui River launched an attack on Wanganui and were stopped at Moutoa Island by Maori from the area around the township. Fifty Upper Wanganui Maori were killed in the fighting before they were driven off. The Lower Wanganui Maori were also involved in the campaigning against the Ngati Ruanui chief Titokowaru, which will be discussed later.

Many Maori also saw the advantage of fighting alongside the Pakeha when settling old scores against traditional enemies — in many cases this could be achieved while on the government payroll. Some also believed that assisting the New Zealand government would protect their own land from confiscation; although as it turned out the initial boundaries drawn in land confiscation seldom took Maori loyalty into consideration. Certainly the involvement of kupapa or 'loyal Maori' depended on their circumstances at any given time, and the level of involvement of these groups varied accordingly.

It seems safe to say, though, that without the help of kupapa many of the campaigns would have been a lot more difficult, and in some cases impossible for the imperial and colonial armies to carry out.

In April 1864 the Arawa tribe entered the war in an effort to protect their own lands from invasion. From the European point of view this was to be one of the most important engagements involving kupapa (Maori fighting on the side of the Queen).

Throughout the Waikato war as the King Movement grew, support came from many tribes across the country, in particular from Opotiki and the East Cape as far as Gisborne.

Seven or eight hundred warriors from these tribes had massed, and requested permission to travel through the Arawa country around Rotorua and join up with the Waikato tribes. This was flatly refused. Invasion of Arawa territory by tribes from the East Coast now seemed likely. At the time, many Arawa were scattered across the northern half of the North Island: they were involved in gumdigging and various other commercial operations. When the news of the apparently imminent invasion reached them, the Arawa abandoned these ventures and returned to protect their home lands. They came in their own fleet of boats and ships, and anchored at Maketu. These vessels were abandoned and many rotted and sank over the several years of fighting that followed; a sandbank formed around the wrecks and nearly ruined the harbour.

The first problem facing the Arawa was the lack of guns and ammunition. They approached the magistrate at Maketu for help. He refused, but William Mair, a government military interpreter and recently appointed resident magistrate at Taupo, realised the importance of stopping 800 armed warriors from joining the Waikato war effort and agreed to help. He approached the military authorities at Tauranga and secured from them their entire supply of sporting ammunition along with three hundredweight of gunpowder and thousands of percussion caps. Lead from any available source was melted down and made into bullets.

The Arawa were reinforced by Rawiri Kahia and Hohepa Tamamutu and their contingent from Taupo, and the combined force of about 400 men swept down the length

Panorama of Lake Rotoiti, which carried the Arawa war canoes to engage the East Coast tribes in 1864.

of Lake Rotoiti in war canoes, the largest of which, *Te Arawa*, could carry 100 men. On the southern shores of the lake they engaged the East Coast tribes. Three days of heavy skirmishing followed, starting on 7 April 1864, in which the invaders were forced to retire. In doing so they announced their intention of invading Maketu.

Maketu was lightly garrisoned by a body of troops under Major Colvile (43rd Regiment) as well as 14 men of the Forest Rangers and Colonial Defence Force under the command of Major Drummond Hay, and Captain Thomas McDonnell, who had recently arrived in order to organise the Arawa defence.

On 21 April 1864 Major Colvile, Ensign H. Hay (Waikato Militia) and Private Key (43rd light infantry) were enjoying a spot of duckshooting on the Waihi lagoon, about two miles east of Maketu, when they suddenly became the hunted. The East Coast tribes, reinforced by another 60 men from Tuhoe and Ngai Tama, had marched on Maketu and, on seeing the duckshooters, had opened fire. Major Colvile and co paddled their own canoe as fast as they were able and made a lucky escape into the surrounding bush.

Skirmishing followed for the next two days and the East Coast army entrenched themselves below the Maketu fort, but were forced to abandon this position after being shelled by the warship *Falcon* and the gunboat *Sandfly*. They made their way across the lagoon and occupied the sandhills on the east side. This position was stormed by the Arawa, assisted by a few men from the Forest Rangers and the Colonial Defence Force Cavalry.

Maketu.

The East Coast army retreated and were chased along the beach, with the *Falcon* and the *Sandfly* sailing down the coast, shelling them on the way.

A final stand was made near the Puakowhai Stream. The Arawa made a series of charges at the new position in between volleys and eventually broke through the line of defence. The chase resumed and the battle did not finish until the invaders reached Matata, where they made their escape by canoe towards Whakatane.

I dragged myself out of a warm bed at Taupo well before sunrise — I wanted to photograph Lake Rotoiti in the first light of the day. Getting out of bed is not something I'm good at, and I considered myself a real hero as I drove towards the lake. When I got there I found that I could have stayed in bed: it was a dull overcast sort of day, in spite of the fact that the previous two days had been brilliantly clear. I promised myself I'd do early evening shooting in future.

But as I gazed out over Rotoiti I saw in my mind's eye the war canoes advancing out of the mist with paddles pushing through the water, and I could just about hear the war cries of those on board. As I came back to reality, I was greeted with a clear silence interrupted only by the sound of a single voice singing. I turned around, trying to find the source of this beautiful sound, but I could see no one. Somewhere in the community of Hinehopu on the shores of Lake Rotoiti is a woman who has considerable musical talent.

Volkner

The Pai Marire religion was founded in 1862 by Te Ua Haumene, from the Taranaki tribe south of New Plymouth, on the basis of a visitation from the Angel Gabriel. The religion was a mixture of Old Testament Christianity and traditional Maori beliefs. Te Ua, who saw a direct relationship between the Maori people and the Jews, chose Jehovah as the religion's main deity. Also emphasised were the twin gods of war and peace, Rura and Riki, though Pai Marire, which translates as 'good and peaceful', was pacifist in principle. Another thing that was strongly emphasised was the importance of holding the land, selling it was vigorously opposed.

From 1864 the new religion spread across the country and was eagerly accepted by many Maori, who were becoming increasingly disenchanted with Christianity and all things 'Pakeha'. Kereopa was one of the missionaries sent to spread the word. His arrival in Opotiki was to coincide with the return of Volkner to Opotiki.

When I was a kid I was told, as part of my education, that in March 1865 a nice missionary chap by the name of Volkner was brutally murdered by a band of bloodthirsty fanatics. His murderers were followers of the Pai Marire religion — or should I say, 'cult' — also known as Hauhauism. The Hauhaus strung Volkner up from a tree outside his own church. Before he was dead they cut him down, disembowelled him, cut off his head and swallowed his eyes. A chalice from the church was filled with his blood and passed round the congregation, who greedily drank it all up. That is why, we were told, these Hauhaus had to be stopped.

In the course of researching this book I discovered that the only fact in this story is the date, though it seems likely that Volkner was beheaded in accordance with a traditional Maori insult. My suspicions were aroused when I found that the person who wrote the report of Volkner's death wasn't there when it happened.

St Stephen's Anglican Church, Opotiki, the church of Volkner.

Reverend Carl Sylvius Volkner had been the resident missionary at what is now known as St Stephen's Church in Opotiki for four years and had been made a member of the Whakatohea people. When war broke out, Volkner, like many other missionaries in the country, turned on the very people whom he had claimed to love: in short, he became a spy. In letters to Governor Grey he sent strategic information, and details of who was in the Opotiki area and what they were doing there.

He was found out, and when he went to Auckland to remove his wife to safety he was sent a message from the Whakatohea warning him of the consequences if he returned.

Volkner chose to ignore this advice and insisted on returning to Opotiki. With him was another missionary, Thomas Grace, and they arrived on the coastal trader *Eclipse*, a

Inside St Stephen's, Opotiki.

schooner owned and under the command of Captain Levy and his partner Morris. Only Volkner and Grace went ashore. Volkner was seized, and Grace was placed in loose confinement and eventually allowed to escape — which action in itself does not conform to the behaviour of bloodthirsty fanatics.

Volkner was confronted by his accusers and, being unable to defend his actions, was sentenced — customary to Maori law at that time (and European law, for that matter) — to death. He was taken to a nearby willow, and a rope was thrown over one of the branches. Volkner prayed, then the sentence was carried out.

The report that carried details of all the atrocities that followed was written by the owners of the *Eclipse*. Perhaps they could have helped Volkner but chose not to, either out of fear for their own safety or out of concern for their trading business in the Opotiki area. It seems certain that they themselves were not in danger, as they were both Jews and, as such, were looked upon kindly. Their report of the incident did nothing, however, for the reputation of the Pai Marire followers. As Pai Marire was gaining popularity among the Maori, wild stories of barbaric practices were spread about. These increased the settlers' fear and made them determined to crush what they saw as a threat to their own authority.

Omaranui

I drove out of Napier heading south, looking for the Omaranui Pa site. When I found Omaranui Road I knew that I was close; and the monument erected in 1916 commemorating the battle confirmed that I was close. But what I was really looking for was the ground where the fighting took place. As I stood on the road beside the Longridge vineyards and gazed out past the long lines of grapes, I could see nothing that was an obvious pa site. I decided to head back into Taupo, get some lunch and check out the local museum.

While I was going through some old photographs at the museum, I asked a member of the staff about Omaranui. She wasn't sure of the exact location herself; but as we were talking I noticed a bloke looking at me sideways, one eyebrow raised, with a 'What's going on here? Looks like he's from Auckland' kind of expression. He introduced himself: he was Dan Panapa, direct descendant of the Pai Marire prophet Panapa who died at Omaranui during the battle. As it turned out, Dan was doing some research for a book of his own, and he agreed to show me the site.

We went out to take a look around. When Dan showed me the pa site, I wasn't surprised that I had missed it. From a distance it didn't look like much — just a small hill among other small hills. But as I got close, that feeling that I was having more and more as I travelled the country started kicking in: this was another very special place. It was getting on toward late afternoon by this stage, and Dan asked if I would mind not taking photographs right now, as it was spiritually healthier to take them in the morning. The evening was a sad time, a time when the dead were buried. Morning would bring a new beginning.

The next morning at first light we returned to Omaranui. A road was being built past the site, and the surrounding area was being subdivided into 10-acre blocks, but the hill on which the events had taken place was left alone — well, just about alone. As I moved around the perimeter of the hill, checking out angles and light, I became aware of bone chips scattered on the ground. I thought nothing of it until Dan picked up a bone and said, 'What do you think this is?' He reckoned it was a bone from a forearm, and I couldn't think what else it

Omaranui Pa.

might have been. There were other bones, including what looked like the jawbone of a child. It appeared that a bulldozer working close to the site had turned a graveyard upside down. It was a sad thought. Dan said it would be taken care of — and a couple of months later he rang and told me that things had been put to rights.

Dan's ancestor, the prophet Panapa, came with a small army of about 80 from his village of Te Haroto, which is on the Napier–Taupo road, into the Napier area. According to the history books, his intention was to sack the town of Napier, though according to Dan Panapa the intention was to continue on to the old pa of Roto-a-Kiwa and talk to the people there about holding onto what land was left, and to obtain guns and ammunition from them. Whatever the intention, the people of Napier feared it was an invasion.

A government interpreter called F.E. Hamlin was sent out to meet the prophet and tell him to go home, but there was no response to this request. At midnight on 11 October 1866, about 200 local militia and volunteer cavalry marched out of Napier and made their way to the fenced village of Omaranui. The militia were under the command of

Colonel George Whitmore, who had served under General Cameron, and had since taken up farming in the Napier area. He had now come out of retirement and, as we shall see, was to be very busy for the next few years.

When Whitmore's troops arrived at Omaranui, Panapa was told to surrender. When no response was forthcoming, Whitmore sent two companies across the river that ran in front of the pa. As the men crossed the river they could have easily come under attack from the pa, as they were out in the open. Under orders from the Pai Marire leader they were not fired on, and the troops moved into position in safety. They then opened fire on three sides of the pa.

Some of Panapa's men came out into the open and attempted to skirmish their way forward. This move was unsuccessful and many, including Panapa, were killed. The rest sought the scant protection offered by the whare and meeting house. After about an hour they realised the hopelessness of their position and tried to escape out the back way. At this point the cavalry sprang into action and rounded up most of the survivors.

After the battle, the wounded were taken to Napier and treated at the local hospital. Many of the prisoners were shipped to the penal settlement in the Chatham Islands, where they joined Te Kooti and his followers.

Te Kooti

WAERENGA-A-HIKA

There are no obvious signs at Waerenga-a-Hika that a battle was once fought there that took the lives of over 100 men. Once again I found myself driving up and down a short length of road saying to myself, 'Where is it?' There is a great-looking hotel on the corner of the road leading into Waerenga-a-Hika, so that seemed a good place to make some enquiries. The hotel manager pointed out a house and said that a fellow named Jim lived there and had been in the area for a long time, so he would be my best bet.

I knocked on Jim Brown's door and asked him if he knew where the Waerenga-a-hika Pa site was. 'Yeah,' he said. 'It's right outside my kitchen window.' I had found another friend.

Panorama of the area surrounding Mohaka, where raids were carried out by Te Kooti.

Jim Brown had grown up in the area. He told me that, as a kid, he used to play in the remnants of the old trenches. Before long we had books, maps and papers covering his table and he was pointing out all the bits to me. 'That's where the old mission house was; over there is the graveyard; and the trenches ran past here . . .'

I had to use my imagination — all I could see were some nicely ploughed fields.

Jim offered to lend me his gumboots (I had my Auckland shoes on) so I could have a look around and take some photographs. In the meantime he checked out some of the written accounts of the battle I had with me. He said on my return that some of the information he found a bit confusing, compared to what he had grown up believing. We parted company agreeing that written history is a funny thing.

One thing is for sure, there was nothing funny about Waerenga-a-Hika in November of 1865.

Waerenga-a-Hika had become the centre of Maori resistance in the Gisborne area. A pa had been built there by Pai Marire followers, and in November 1865, 150–200 colonial troops and another 300 or so kupapa turned up to crush the rebellion.

Most of the buildings in the area had been destroyed, and it was the arrival of the colonial troops that saved the mission house. For the colonials this was fortuitous, because the mission house was within rifle range of the pa and was being used as a position for sharpshooters — a few of the weatherboards around the upstairs part of the house had been removed for this purpose.

The remains of Waerenga-a-hika photographed in 1866. Hawke's Bay Museum.

Waerenga-a-hika.

The colonial and kupapa troops took up positions covering three sides of the pa and firing started. It was the beginning of a siege that would last a week, during which, as we shall see, some of the Maori loyal to the Queen were more loyal than others.

Lieutenant Wilson and 30 military settlers moved around to the north side of the pa and a sap was started. As it got close to the pa they came under attack from reinforcements which had arrived from a neighbouring village. Wilson and his men had found themselves virtually surrounded, so the order was given to 'fix bayonets and charge'. By concentrating their efforts on the bulk of the attackers, Wilson's men managed to break through and drive the attack off. This was achieved at a cost — six men died and five more were wounded.

The next day was Sunday, and after a Pai Marire service, three columns of Maori streamed out of the pa and attacked the Hawke's Bay Militia who had taken up a position behind a hawthorn hedge. The Pai Marire followers, possibly full of religious fervour, threw themselves into the attack and did not withdraw until about 60 of them had been killed.

Many of the colonial and kupapa soldiers who witnessed the attack were under the impression that the attackers came carrying white flags of truce; but they chose not to trust them, and opened fire anyway. It seems more likely that the flags they were carrying were white with a red cross and/or a crescent moon in the corner — Pai Marire fighting flags.

The officer in command of the colonial forces, Major James Fraser, had at his disposal one six-pounder that had been brought ashore from the steamer *Sturt*. On the seventh day of fighting, he decided to use it. There was no conventional ammunition for the gun, so a couple of salmon tins filled with shrapnel were fired into the pa. They probably caused little damage, but in spite of this a white flag appeared from inside the pa and the battle was over. Some of the garrison had escaped into the surrounding swamp, but the majority surrendered.

Up until recently it was the view of historians that the two salmon tins of shrapnel fired into the pa were the cause of the surrender, but as James Belich points out in *The New Zealand Wars*, this seems unlikely. Those inside the pa had been under siege for a week, and had stood up to all that was thrown at them. Two salmon tins of shrapnel exploding in the pa would hardly have been enough to convince the Pai Marire to surrender, unless it was felt that this was the beginning of a much larger bombardment, one which they would be unable to withstand.

Throughout the conflict there was much dissatisfaction among the colonial troops as to the conduct of the kupapa. It seems that ammunition and information were smuggled into the pa; and the involvement of many of the Maori fighting on the side of the colonials was less than enthusiastic. The possible reasons for this have already been pointed out; but at Waerenga-a-Hika, some kupapa were suspected of treason. Among them was Te Kooti Arikirangi Te Turuki.

Te Kooti was from the Rongowhakaata tribe, and was born in 1830. He had received some education at the mission station at Waerenga-a-Hika, and it's possible that he was literate in both Maori and English, which was unusual for the times. He has been described as a wild man in his youth, and had made several enemies in the Poverty Bay area where he lived. For a start he was involved in a trading operation that put him in direct competition with a leading businessman of the district, one Captain Read. He had also apparently seduced the wives of some of the Maori chiefs, and this did nothing for his popularity.

The initial charges against Te Kooti, of spying at Waerenga-a-Hika, were dropped. He was also accused of firing blanks during the battle, and this was possibly true — his brother Komene was one of those in the pa. But these charges too were dropped, due to lack of evidence, and he was set free — only to be rearrested later on and accused of further treason.

Te Kooti was regarded by many as a troublemaker, and it seems certain that his eventual deportation to the Chatham Islands was due to trumped-up charges laid against him by those who wanted him out of the way. He demanded a trial but this was denied him and he was bundled onto a boat to be taken out to the steamer *St Kilda* that was to transport him to the Chatham Islands with Pai Marire prisoners captured at Waerenga-a-Hika. As he got on the boat he protested his innocence, and one of those present, Paratene Pototi, showed his contempt for Te Kooti by mimicking the Pakeha officers around him, saying 'Go ona te poti (go on the boat).' It was an insult that would be remembered.

CHATHAM ISLANDS

There were four batches of prisoners transported to the Chatham Islands. The incarceration of these men and the families that were allowed to go with them was illegal, and was later on recognised as such. It was a grim existence that awaited them. They were for the most part poorly clothed, and the colder climate took its toll. When they arrived on the Chathams after a harsh 500-mile voyage, there was no housing prepared and they had to set to work to provide their own. Buildings were constructed from whatever materials were available — mostly ponga logs and flax. Initially they were given government rations, but it was expected that crops would be grown to supplement and eventually replace this food source. They were given spades, shovels and picks with which to farm, and later they were provided with ploughs. These were pulled by the prisoners, as well as by their wives and children. This was a humiliation that all of them felt. Fishing was another source of food, but they were not used to the wild Chatham Island coast, and found it difficult.

The 25 guards who watched over them were a mixed bunch: some were fair, but there

Pai Marire prisoners destined for the Chathams, November 1865. Hawke's Bay Museum.

were incidents of brutality and some of the women were molested. On top of all this, the resident doctor turned out to be a man who liked a drink, and was often unable to perform his duties as a result.

There was a lot of sickness; and one of those who fell ill was Te Kooti. The medical records state that he had chronic asthma, but judging by the symptoms it is more likely that he had tuberculosis. At one point it seemed that he was going to die, and preparations were made for his funeral. He recovered, however, and it was during the peak of his fever that he experienced a series of visions on which he based the Ringatu religion. Ringatu, meaning upraised hand, was a mixture of Old Testament and traditional Maori beliefs, and was similar in many respects to Pai Marire, except that Te Kooti added his own variations.

Te Kooti was a charismatic man. He was also very intelligent. It was these qualities, as well as the new religion, which gave him a great deal of respect amongst the prisoners on the island: although he had no inherited mana, there were several chiefs there who were happy to submit to his authority. The prisoners on the Chatham Islands became the first of many Ringatu converts, and Te Kooti became their leader.

The term of imprisonment was to be two years with good behaviour; but as the two-year mark approached, there was no indication of their impending release. Te Kooti decided therefore that they would release themselves. He devised a complex plan of escape.

On 4 July 1868 there were two boats moored at Waitangi Bay in the Chatham Islands

— the ketch *Florence* and a three-masted schooner called *Rifleman*. Several groups of prisoners overpowered the crew of the *Rifleman* and at the same time seized the guard house and captured the redoubt. Forty guns were taken, as well as 4000 rounds of ammunition. The commanding officer, Captain Thomas, was forced to hand over the keys to the safe and was bound hand and foot. The safe was emptied: the money from it, added to the cash taken from the guards and others, came to 522 pounds. One of Te Kooti's lieutenants, Peka Makarini (Baker McLean) appropriated a bugle, which he used to good effect during the fighting that followed by sending out calls and confusing the colonial troops. On one occasion, when he knew that the soldiers were hungry and short of rations, he repeatedly sent out the mess call. Makarini had a reputation as a fierce fighter; it seems he also had a sense of humour.

The captain of the *Rifleman* was left at Waitangi Bay and the ship set sail for home. On board were 163 men, 64 women and 71 children as well as the *Rifleman*'s crew, who were assisted by some of the prisoners who had sailing experience. It was a hard voyage. The weather turned nasty and the ship was forced to tack constantly in an effort to make headway into the wind. After three days they were still about 100 miles from the coast of New Zealand and battling their way through the storm. At this point Te Kooti ordered that an elderly relative of his, Te Warihi, be brought up on deck and thrown overboard as a sacrifice to God. Te Warihi had been accused of giving information to the authorities at Waitangi Bay and Te Kooti had intended to execute him on reaching the mainland anyway. He was lifted over the rails and dropped into the sea. He 'sank like a stone'. Not long after the execution the weather improved and the ship delivered its cargo at Whareongaonga on 9 July 1868.

The ship was unloaded and the next day Te Kooti paid six pounds to each of the crew and said they could come with him if they wanted. The crew turned the offer down and instead sailed the *Rifleman* to Wellington.

Te Kooti headed inland with the intention of reaching the safety of Puketapu, near Lake Waikaremoana. Just before he left Whareongaonga he received a visit from a government emissary telling him to surrender. Te Kooti refused, saying that he would not fight unless attacked — he just wanted to be left alone. The colonial authorities found his response unacceptable, and three columns were quickly organised for the pursuit.

The first column, under the command of Major R. Biggs and consisting of 66 colonial troops and 22 kupapa, engaged Te Kooti's forces at Paparatu on 20 July. The second column under Captain W. A. Richardson and made up of 25 colonials and 100 kupapa had a minor engagement on 24 July at Te Koneke. The third and final column, consisting of 30 colonial soldiers and 40 kupapa with Colonel G.S. Whitmore, who had overall command, met up with the escaped prisoners at Ruakituri. All three of these engagements failed in their objective to stop Te Kooti — each time they were fought off, in spite of the fact that Te Kooti had no more than 50 armed warriors. Te Kooti was displaying yet another talent, that of guerrilla warfare. Casualties suffered by Te Kooti's forces were light, though he himself received an ankle wound during the fight at Ruakituri.

When he reached Puketapu, Te Kooti started a recruitment drive. Messages seeking support were sent over a wide area. The response, however, wasn't great — he received a lot of sympathy, but what he really needed was men, guns and ammunition. By the time he was ready to move on, some two months later, he had about 250 warriors, 20 per cent of whom were unarmed.

Over on the west coast of the North Island another war was brewing, involving Titokowaru in southern Taranaki. On 7 September the colonial troops had suffered a huge defeat at Te Ngutu-o-te-Manu, and troops from the East Coast had been sent there to deal with the problem. In what was probably an effort to avoid fighting two wars at once, a secret government emissary, the Reverend Rainier, was sent to find Te Kooti and make an offer of peace.

The terms were that if the Chatham Island prisoners surrendered, no further measures would be taken against them; and they would be found some land on which to live. Te Kooti had just spent two years in prison without trial, and was understandably suspicious: he turned down the offer without giving it much consideration.

MATAWHERO

There had been rumours that Wairoa could be the scene of an attack by Te Kooti, and troops had been moved into the area. It's more than likely that Te Kooti started the rumour: instead he moved his people to the neutral village of Patutahi. Once there he took the inhabitants prisoner, so that word of his arrival wouldn't get out; and on 9 November he moved down onto the plains below to the settlement of Matawhero with 100 hand-picked warriors. For the time being, at least, he had stopped running.

Major Reginald Biggs, the colonist-commander living at Matawhero, was well aware of the possibility of an attack by Te Kooti. He had his own spies working in the area, and he was convinced that if the attack did come, it would be from the south. He had positioned his nine scouts accordingly, under the command of Lieutenant Gascoyne. So confident was he that he felt it unnecessary to move the inhabitants of the area into the Turanganui redoubt. The major's spies may have been double agents, or Te Kooti may have deliberately spread false information: when the attack came, it came from the west via a disused overgrown track.

Te Kooti had his reasons for attacking Matawhero. Success here would seriously disrupt the colonial defence — and the raid could easily be justified on these grounds — but the killings that took place were also selective, and many of them were of a personal nature. Te Kooti held Major Biggs as one of those most responsible for his illegal imprisonment, so from a military and a personal point of view, Biggs' chances didn't look good.

Te Kooti had also owned land at Matawhero, but during his imprisonment the land had become subject to some shady dealings, and he lost it while he was absent and unable to defend the title. Part of the land became the property of Captain Read, the trader, and some passed into the hands of some of the local Maori. Te Kooti had a few scores to settle.

The Ringatu warriors moved into Matawhero shortly before midnight on 9 November 1868. They had been split up into smaller groups and sent to specific targets. A group led by one of Te Kooti's lieutenants, Te Rangitahau, came to Major Biggs' house and fired volleys into it. The door was then broken down, and Biggs and his wife and child and others were taken outside and shot, then bayoneted. Te Rangitahau then moved off in the direction of Captain Wilson's home. He set fire to the house, rounded up the Wilsons

Modern-day Patutahi.

This church at Matawhero was the only building left standing after Te Kooti's raid.

and led them outside. Captain Wilson was carrying his infant son, James, in his arms when he was killed. His wife and children were also stabbed, and the three children died; but his wife, who had been left for dead, survived for a few days. The infant James escaped unhurt and wandered around in a daze for two days before finding his badly wounded mother, who had made her way into a shed. She wrote a note and gave it to the boy, telling him to find help. The poor little chap got lost, and eventually turned up at Makaraka. His mother was rescued by a search party and taken to the hospital at Napier, where she died from her wounds.

The attack was a total surprise. Te Kooti was outnumbered and most of the settlers in the area were armed, but before the night was through Te Kooti controlled the whole area and had killed 34 Europeans and another 22 Maori, including Piripi Taketake and his family. Taketake and his wife Harata Poharu were involved in the dispute over Te Kooti's land at Matawhero, and had been taken prisoner during the raid. Te Kooti had them and their five children separated from the other prisoners and shot then bayoneted. 'God has told me to kill women and children. Fire on them,' he declared. He then ordered Psalm 63:10 ('They shall fall by the sword') to be sung, before moving off with the rest of the prisoners towards Patutahi, leaving the bodies where they lay. The only building left standing after the raid was the church — the rest were burned to the ground.

Te Kooti, using Patutahi as a base, stayed in the area for the next week rounding up huge numbers of horses and cattle as well as about 300 Maori whom he took as prisoners. Somewhere between 20 and 40 of these unfortunate people, including women and children, were executed. Of the rest about 100 were starved to death and many others were killed by colonial soldiers, as they were mistaken for Ringatu followers during subsequent battles. Also taken were about 100 rifles and some ammunition.

MAKARETU

On 17 November Te Kooti withdrew from Poverty Bay, making his way to Makaretu about 30 miles away. On his trail were about 450 Maori from the Ngati Kahungunu and Rongowhakaata tribes, as well as Lieutenant Gascoyne and eight Europeans. On reaching Makaretu they engaged the Ringatu army and were confident of success. Te Kooti's position did not appear to be a strong one and he could not move quickly with about 400 non-combatants, not to mention sheep, cattle and various other plunder. He was also short of ammunition, as what he had taken from the Matawhero raid did not amount to much.

In spite of these problems, Te Kooti counter-attacked and drove off several charges. During one of these he set fire to the surrounding bush, making things pretty hot for the kupapa and their allies. Both sides dug in and a stalemate went on for three days. The kupapa were still willing to continue the attack, but had to wait for ammunition and food to be brought up from a depot at Patutahi.

Te Kooti also knew about the depot and launched a daring raid against it. Although the raid was a small one it was swift and beautifully done. Twenty chosen men on horseback led by Peka Makarini charged the 25 Pakeha and kupapa guarding the supplies, forcing them to flee. The Ringatu raiders got away with over 12,000 rounds of much-needed ammunition and destroyed all that they could not carry.

In the meantime reinforcements, in the form of 370 men from Ngati Kahungunu and Ngati Porou tribes, including Ropata Wahawaha, arrived at Makaretu, bringing badly needed supplies and ammunition. On 3 December this combined force, now about 800 strong, launched a full-scale attack and Makaretu was taken. It was a hollow victory. Te Kooti had left, taking with him his prisoners and livestock and leaving behind a rear guard of between 50 to 80 men. The rear guard fought bravely and long enough to ensure Te Kooti's escape, though in the process at least 14 were killed. Te Kooti made his way to his next stronghold, at Ngatapa.

Officially the action at Makaretu was celebrated as a victory. In reality, it was a bitter disappointment.

Te Kooti

NGATAPA

In the course of putting together this book there are some things that I had to learn the hard way. One of them was to do the research before I charged off around the country, cameras in hand. I had been through the Gisborne area before but had failed to find the Ngatapa mountain. Later on, back in Auckland, I came across a sentence in Belich's The New Zealand Wars *that gave me a clue as to where this place might be. When I was next in South Taranaki I decided to return home the long way and have another go at finding Ngatapa.*

After driving most of the day, I hit Gisborne and immediately headed inland in what I thought was the right direction. As I drove through the drought-stricken and rugged hill country I caught a glimpse of the mountain. I slammed on the anchors and was gazing at this sharp and sinister peak when a local farmer came out of his house, wandered over and said 'Gidday.' I asked him if that was in fact Ngatapa — I had to be sure. He said it was, and would I like to go and have a closer look? He gave me directions to the owners of the land where the peak was: 'You go down there, cross a couple of bridges, past the woolshed on the right . . .'

I found the place, walked up the driveway and met Mr and Mrs Jobson. One of the things that has amazed me in the course of gathering photos for this book has been the warmth and hospitality of the people I've had the good fortune to meet. Reid and his wife were certainly no exception. 'Hello,' I said to them, 'I'm Neil Finlay and I'm doing this book . . .' Within two minutes I was sitting in the living room with a cup of tea, doing one of the things I enjoy most — watching the cricket on tv — and feeling right at home.

As it turned out, the Ngatapa peak was on the neighbouring property, but a phone call was made and I had permission to go up. Reid gave me directions: 'See that path going past the pine trees? Follow that, go up there, round there . . .' It was obvious that I had a long uphill walk in front of me, but I had come a long way already and this was just too good to miss. Nathan Astle was batting and appeared to be doing all right when he was stumped, out for 30-something, and I took this as my cue to get started. By the time I had got my camera gear out of the car and come back to the house, two more wickets had fallen and things were looking bad for the Kiwi cricket team. Reid said, 'Hang on a minute and I'll give you a ride up.' He probably guessed that I hadn't run any marathons lately, and either took pity on me or figured that if I expired on his property from heat and exhaustion, he'd be left to clean up the mess.

He filled up the tank of his four-wheel-drive motorcycle and off we went. We roared, stumbled and bounced over the steep landscape, with me hanging on to my camera bag with one hand and dear life with the other, as I sat side-saddle on the back of this remarkable little machine. We eventually reached the base of Ngatapa and went virtually straight up, along a very narrow track strewn with rocks that had fallen down from above. At one point Reid said, 'You don't want to look down as we go over this next bit.' I did look down, and he was right — I didn't want to.

Ngatapa, looking down over the 'women's retreat' and the escape route to the right.

We spiralled our way round to the face of the hill up the final slope and we were there. Ngatapa rises about 245 metres (800 feet) from the base of the hills on which it sits and once at the top you are over 610 metres (2000 ft) above sea level. The view is fantastic, spreading off to the coast about 40 kilometres away to the east and to the Ureweras on the other side. Reid gave me a guided tour around the site, and with his help I could put into place the terrible events that occurred here just over 120 years ago.

We sat around for a while and chatted about farming and droughts and stuff, and Reid pointed out several homes in the area that had burnt down in fairly recent times. We could see a storm coming in from the distance but it eventually went around us; apparently there wasn't enough rain in it to make any difference anyway. We shoved off and roared, stumbled and bounced our way back down towards the house. At one point Reid said, 'A second-class ride is better than a first-class walk.'

For me this was, most definitely, a first-class ride.

Te Kooti moved to his next position, Ngatapa, an old pa site that sat on the top of a high hill about three miles from Makaretu. The pa was triangular in shape with the apex

Ngatapa, looking down over the 'Crow's Nest'.

at the top leading to an escape route of sorts via a ridge extending down into the surrounding mountainous country. The only logical approach to the pa was along the main ridge to the top of the hill, via a smaller hill referred to as the 'Crow's Nest'.

The pa had its good and bad points. The water supply came from two small springs which, though not inside the pa itself, were protected by a series of outer earthworks. The approach to the pa was extremely difficult due to the steep rugged terrain, but escape could also be difficult. Whitmore realised, after an initial attack led by the gallant and ruthless Major Ropata, that the pa might not be able to be stormed but it could, with difficulty, be virtually surrounded.

Ropata's attack came on 4 December as Te Kooti was working quickly to fortify the pa. The main defences were three long parapets and trenches built parallel to each other and extending across the front of the pa. These parapets were to protect the huts behind them and, as it turned out, were too wide for rifle fire to be angled to cover the ground directly in front. Surrounding the pa and covering access to it was a series of rifle pits. There were also bunkers to protect the inhabitants from shell fire, but these lacked the necessary depth to absorb the blast. Te Kooti was, without a doubt, a brilliant guerrilla fighter, but he was not skilled in fortifying a defensive position. This was to be a test that he would fail — twice.

Major Ropata Wahawaha was not to have everything his way either. After an initial attack he managed to get into a trench on the front left of the pa, not far from the front wall. From this position he commenced firing along the trench as fast as he could, with the assistance of Lieutenant Preece. The bulk of the attacking forces, consisting mainly of Ngati Porou from Wairoa, however, had been forced back as a result of a counter-attack and had repositioned themselves around a warm fire about 500 yards away. Ropata had sent messages to these men demanding assistance, but his demands met with little enthusiasm. Some agreed to move up and help the following morning, but by this time Ropata and Preece had expended their ammunition and given up in disgust. There was no victory for Ropata that day — but things were not much better for Te Kooti. In the fighting that had taken place since the raid on Matawhero, he had lost at least 57 men, and about 60 rifles had been captured.

For their efforts Ropata and Preece were awarded the New Zealand Cross.

While I was visiting the museum at Napier I had a rare and brief opportunity to look over some of Colonel Whitmore's personal belongings. One of the things I picked up was a journal. In between its blank pages was a collection of pressed plants and flowers. It was a very pretty collection and as I looked through it, I was a little taken aback. Collections such as these may have been a popular hobby of the times, but everything I had learnt about Colonel Whitmore suggested that he was not a man who would go around picking flowers.

Colonel George Stoddart Whitmore, like Lt-General Cameron, was a very competent military commander; but whereas Cameron had a certain amount of compassion and understanding of the people he was fighting, Whitmore was less inclined to care. He was a hard man, hated and feared by those he fought and by those he commanded. The press gave him a rough time, as did most of the local dignitaries, who described him as a 'contemptible little brute', 'a chip of the devil' or 'a little conceited, egotistical, self sufficient ass', and so on. Whitmore nevertheless earned some respect for his ability as a soldier.

Whitmore arrived at Poverty Bay in early December and wanted to attack Te Kooti before he moved out of his stronghold at Ngatapa. In order to achieve this he had to amass enough troops to besiege the pa, and equip them with food and ammunition. Major Ropata and his Ngati Porou troops had returned to Waiapu to refit; and Donald McLean, a local official and much-loved resident of Poverty Bay, refused to cooperate with Whitmore, and cost him valuable manpower. A feud was being carried on between Whitmore and McLean and, although it was mainly a war of words, it put the whole campaign in jeopardy.

McLean persuaded about 700 Ngati Kahungunu to mount their own campaign against Te Kooti. The Ngati Kahungunu expedition came to nothing, and it diverted men whom Whitmore could have used. Eventually recruits came, including a constabulary division of 60 Arawa from Tauranga. These men brought Whitmore's force up to 320, and on Christmas Eve 1868 they marched to within three miles of the Ngatapa fortress and waited there for Ropata to join them. Ropata was ill at the time and his advance was slow, but on 30 December he arrived, and the process of surrounding the pa could begin.

On the last day of 1868 Colonel Whitmore and Major Ropata Wahawaha moved their force onto the lower hill, the Crow's Nest, down the ridge from the pa. The Crow's Nest became the base of operations, and from there detachments were sent out to surround the pa as best they could. Te Kooti had his sharpshooters covering the approaches to the pa and the rugged country meant that any movement forward had to be taken slowly and carefully. To make things worse for defenders and attackers alike, it started to rain: the rifle pits and trenches turned to mud and the slopes surrounding the pa became even more treacherous. The main ridge extending from the Crow's Nest to the pa had been blocked, sealing the most obvious route of escape — though there were others.

Major Ropata cut off any escape from the base of the triangular pa, and in so doing he also cut off the water supply. Four men who had come down from the pa to the springs were captured and shot on the spot. In the meantime Fraser, along with Ropata's co-chief Hotene Porourangi and 100 men, had moved to a position behind the pa and blocked off the ridge that extended in that direction, thus blocking another escape route. They all clung to the side of the mountain and bravely fought off several attacks that came from a stony outcrop at the rear of the pa called the 'Pa Puku' (the women's retreat). The north side of the pa was not occupied, as escape from there was not considered possible.

By the fourth day of the siege the rain started to clear, and a mortar that had been manhandled up to the pa was brought into action. The incline of the pa meant that the gunners could fire shells directly into it, but the shrapnel was hitting the front line of the attackers, so its use was discontinued.

In the early hours of 6 January a woman's voice was heard calling out that the pa had been evacuated. As Whitmore's men entered the fortress they found a small group of women and children and a few wounded. Everybody else — at least 190 people — had escaped by climbing down a cliff on the northwest side of the pa. The route they took was very steep, and vines about 60 feet in length were used to lower them down. Once on solid ground they split up into small groups and fled along many paths through the bush.

Whitmore sent Ropata and the Ngati Porou and Arawa troops in pursuit, and Ropata immediately split his forces into small groups and sent them down the bush tracks. When they returned they had captured about 130 of Te Kooti's followers. These men were marched to the outer parapet of the pa and were shot in batches. This slaughter was carried out by members of Ngati Porou and the Arawa constabulary, and was endorsed by Whitmore and by Native Minister J.C. Richmond. To make matters worse, many of those shot were prisoners taken by Te Kooti during the raid on Poverty Bay. The lack of food and water at the pa meant that the inhabitants were reduced to eating fernroot, and Te Kooti's prisoners would have suffered greatly from starvation: this would have slowed their escape.

Te Kooti himself got away — some say on a mythical white horse. How he escaped was probably not as important as the fact that he had lost two thirds of his fighting force. He was still free, however — and he was to rebuild his army, and use it again.

WHAKATANE

Te Kooti retired to the northern Urewera mountains and kept his head down until he had sorted out his next move. His defeat at Ngatapa was a disaster. He had less than 100 followers left, and of these about 40 were women and children, so his first priority was to regain his fighting numbers and arm them. A few Whakatohea tribesmen from the Whakatane area had joined him during February, and he thought that a raid there would yield more supporters — willing or otherwise. Over the next three years he was to maintain the fight, and many of the prisoners he took eventually fought alongside him, some because they wanted to and some because they thought it unwise not to. A series of random executions provided a compelling argument for cooperation.

The supply of guns and ammunition was another pressing problem. Towards the end of the siege at Ngatapa, Te Kooti's followers were reduced to melting down pewter utensils and anything else that came to hand in order in make bullets.

On 2 March 1869 Te Kooti visited the pa at Ohiwa in a recruitment drive, and got support from several (though not all) of the Tuhoe chiefs and their men. On 9 March he moved out of the Ureweras and advanced on Whakatane. With him were 200 people, all well armed. His objective was the Rauporoa Pa on the west bank of the Whakatane River, home of the Ngati Pukeko.

The war party approached the pa under a flag of truce, but the sight of so many armed men aroused the suspicions of those inside and the gate was quickly shut and a volley sent out to the visitors. Te Kooti's men retreated, found what little cover they could over the flat ground and proceeded to dig themselves in. What followed was a siege that was to last two days before the defenders, having run out of ammunition, were forced to negotiate their way out of the pa, leaving it to Te Kooti.

In the meantime Te Kooti sent a party to attack the mill at Te Poronui. The mill had been built in 1867 as part of a plan by Governor Grey to set local Maori up in agricultural

A monument erected in memory of Jean Guerren in Whakatane, marked by a millstone from his mill.

ventures. The construction and operation of the mill was handled by a Frenchman called Jean Guerren, who had been hired for the job by the Ngati Pukeko. Beside the mill was a small redoubt, and at the time of the attack there were about seven or eight people there, including Guerren's wife Peti (Erihapeti) and her sister Monika.

The raiding party advanced on the mill and redoubt and dug themselves in at a distance of 300 yards to the north. Jean Guerren had a double-barrel gun and a good supply of ammunition, and set about proving his reputation as a 'crack shot'.

This tiny garrison put up a good fight and kept the raiders at bay for two days. The scene must have been reminiscent of an old 'western' movie, except that, as so often happens in real life, the cavalry didn't turn up in time. The raiders led by Wirihana Koikoi, who was to die in the attack, moved to a higher position and, looking down into the redoubt, realised how lightly defended the mill was. They then pressed home the attack by skirmishing right up to the walls and attempting to set fire to a whare at the centre of the redoubt. Jean Guerren was forced to abandon the mill and join the others in the redoubt; and it was there, while he was firing from the gate, that he was shot and killed. The attackers swarmed over the walls and through the gate and set about killing the occupants with tomahawks. Two of the defenders escaped by jumping over the walls. One of these, a fellow called Mauriki, was considered to be a 'half-wit'— but he was bright enough, it would seem, to get away. The other was overtaken and killed.

Guerren's wife Peti and her teenage sister were spared the slaughter that followed and instead were taken by one of the raiders, Te Rangihiroa, to Te Kooti's camp at Raupora. Te Kooti wanted to know where Guerren had kept his supply of gunpowder, and when the information was not forthcoming, he ordered that Te Rangihiroa take Peti as his wife and that Monika be killed. Te Rangihiroa carried out the execution, and Peti remained his wife until she died. The mill and surrounding wheatfields were burned to the ground.

During the second day, news of the siege arrived at Opotiki. Major W.G. Mair dispatched the Opotiki Rangers under the command of Captain Henry Mair and Captain Travers with a detachment of armed constabulary, in all about 80 men. In the meantime Lieutenant Gilbert Mair was racing down the beach on a hired horse to raise help from the Ngati Rangitihi at Matata. It was night time, and as he approached Wairaki the horse ran into some quicksand. When Mair tried to jump off, his head came into sharp contact with his rifle butt. The blow knocked him unconscious and when he came to later, the tide was lapping at his feet. Still dazed, he searched the beach for his horse. He found it, remounted and rode off, reaching Matata just after daylight. Once there he raised 130 men, who then marched to Whakatane.

When the colonial forces arrived at Whakatane they found that Te Kooti had occupied the pa and burnt down the redoubt; he was in complete control of the area and was too strong to attack. Te Kooti moved off subsequently, and on 12 March entered a small pa called Paharakeke on the banks of the Rangitaiki River and made prisoners of the 40 or so inhabitants, including women and children. From there he made his way to Tauaroa, where the colonial and kupapa forces again made contact with him, in an unsuccessful attempt to surround the place. After a day and a night the troops withdrew, as some of the kupapa had decided not to fight. Te Kooti abandoned the pa and made his way back to the Ureweras.

MOHAKA

Going from the suburbs of Auckland to Mohaka is like going to a different country. Between the massive white cliffs on one side of the Mohaka River and the hills leading back to State Highway 2 is a large flat area dotted with homes and farms. It appears to be sparsely populated, and the few inhabitants I saw were going about the place over the dusty roads, often on horseback. I made my way down to the mouth of the river and came across a chap who was spending the hot afternoon catching whitebait. He had set his net in the water and was sitting quietly on the bank. He was very friendly and we chatted about this and that,

Alfred Cooper's 1855 watercolour of Mohaka.

Mohaka as it is today.

but I got the impression that I was ruining his peaceful concentration so I said goodbye and left him to it.

There is a watercolour painting of this place painted by Alfred Cooper, who lived (and died) here in the 1860s. Looking at the painting and comparing it to modern day Mohaka shows that little has changed. There were no commercial buildings so far as I could see, and life here seemed quiet, peaceful and happy.

If Jean Guerren's sister-in-law, Monika, had told Te Kooti where Guerren's supply of gunpowder was kept, her life may have been spared. Instead she took the secret with her to the grave. The powder was in fact buried under the whare in the redoubt beside the mill, and Te Kooti left Whakatane without it. This meant he was still short of ammunition. But an opportunity to solve this problem soon presented itself.

There was a government supply of gunpowder somewhere at Mohaka, and Te Kooti was aware of this. Besides the gunpowder, he was also seeking revenge against the inhabitants of this place, who had fought against him earlier.

The Ureweras provided Te Kooti with an excellent hiding place — he had the support of the Tuhoe, and the rugged terrain made pursuit next to impossible. But his warriors were reduced to two or three rounds of ammunition each, so another raid was planned. He and about 100 men crossed Lake Waikaremoana in canoes. During the crossing one of the canoes overturned, and although those on board were safe, 13 valuable rifles were lost. On reaching the other side, Te Kooti sent part of his force under Te Waru towards Wairoa to create a diversion. The ploy worked, and the Ngati Kahungunu from Mohaka raced to reinforce Wairoa leaving only a dozen or so warriors behind. Mohaka was virtually unprotected.

Te Kooti and the rest of his men moved down the Mohaka River and on 10 April 1869 sacked the village of Arakanihi, leaving behind the bodies of 31 people, mostly women and children. The village was secured so as to provide Te Kooti with an escape route after the raid was completed. From there the war party moved into the outlying area of Mohaka, killing seven people on the way, including John Lavin and Alfred Cooper. Lavin had fought against Te Kooti as a member of the militia, and his death was another score settled. The bodies were run through with bayonets and left lying on the ground.

There were two pa at Mohaka, and these were Te Kooti's main objective. The smaller of the pa, Te Huki, was not well placed in terms of defence, as an attacking force could approach the pa under cover until they got virtually to the walls.

Te Kooti laid siege to Te Huki from the afternoon until the following morning, when negotiations took place for the surrender of the pa, with the safety of its inhabitants guaranteed. Te Kooti and his men were allowed entry into the pa, but as they were entering

The Mohaka River.

one of the inhabitants, Heta Te Wainoho, became suspicious of their behaviour and opened fire. The bullet was aimed at Te Kooti himself, and narrowly missed, passing through his clothing. Genuine or not, the truce was now called off and the slaughter began. By the time it was over Te Kooti and his warriors had killed 26 people, again mostly women and children. He had not found the main store of powder and ammunition, but he had retrieved three barrels of cartridges and with these he turned his attention to the larger of the pa, Hiruharama.

During the first day of the Te Huki siege a relieving force from Wairoa had been ambushed and forced to flee, but another smaller force had broken through Te Kooti's lines. This force consisted of kupapa and a trooper named George Hill. Hill had been sent from Wairoa to reconnoitre Mohaka and, on bringing back the news of the attack, joined the relief party. Having broken through Te Kooti's lines, the relief party reinforced the pa and eventually forced his men back from their advanced positions.

An explosion from Te Huki then confirmed that the remainder of the government ammunition supply was no longer available — it had been buried under one of the houses in the pa. Te Kooti retreated.

Te Kooti had gained some ammunition, but not as much as he hoped for; and he had lost 10 of his men. Some of these casualties occurred when a group of warriors sacked the Mohaka pub and stole a quantity of rum, which they took back with them. A number of those who got drunk on the rum became careless, and were shot when they failed to stay under cover. Te Kooti was furious over this affair — he was not a believer in 'Dutch courage', unlike the imperial troops, who were known to take the occasional drink when in tense situations.

The retreat was a leisurely one, stopping at Arakanihi to finish the rest of the grog before heading back to the sanctuary of the Urewera mountains.

WHITMORE'S UREWERA CAMPAIGN

Colonel Whitmore had come to the conclusion that in order to stop Te Kooti he would have to invade the Ureweras. He hoped to bail up Te Kooti there, or at least make it impossible for him to use these rugged mountains as a haven. For the task Whitmore assembled 1300 men, mainly kupapa, and had them equally divided into three columns. One column, under the command of Lt-Colonel Herrick, was to leave Wairoa and enter the Ureweras from the south, crossing Lake Waikaremoana. This column failed to make any impact on the outcome of the campaign. In order to cross the lake, Herrick's men would need several large boats. Some of these they took with them in sections, and the rest they planned to make on the lake shore. By the time this ambitious task was near completion, the two other columns had finished the work and retired.

Colonel Herrick's expedition to Waikaremoana. Hawke's Bay Museum.

Lake Waikaremoana.

Another column, under the command of Lt-Colonel J.H.H. St John, was to leave from Matata, enter the ranges from the north and meet up with the third column under Whitmore himself at Ruatahuna. Whitmore's column also left from Matata and followed the same route that Te Kooti used after the raid on Whakatane.

As they moved through the mountains they systematically destroyed villages and crops, killing any livestock they found and reducing the Tuhoe to desperate circumstances. Resistance was minimal, with most of the villagers fleeing in front of the advance. There were a few ambushes which cost the invading army a few men, and St John's column lost about a dozen men during heavy fighting at Orangakiwa, a pa that protected the village of Tatahoata. When Whitmore's column reached Te Harema on 6 May 1869, he found that most of the men had left to join Te Kooti — but he attacked anyway. From Te Harema he took 50 prisoners, including 40 women and children, and these people he gave to the Arawa troops so as to destroy the whole subtribe, an act that reinforced his barbaric reputation.

The columns of St John and Whitmore met as planned at Ruatahuna on 8 May and stayed in the area for a few days, carrying out the destruction of neighbouring villages.

Some of Whitmore's kupapa irregulars. Hawke's Bay Museum.

Te Kooti, in the meantime, was on the northern shore of Lake Waikaremoana waiting for Herrick's column to attack. This never happened, and eventually Te Kooti moved off. The only contact he was to have with Whitmore was when his advance guard under Peka Makarini ran into a scouting party. Heavy skirmishing followed in which three of Te Kooti's men were killed, but the expected main attack didn't eventuate. The Arawa troops refused to advance beyond Ruatahuna. There was concern amongst the Arawa about supplies, and about the fact that they weren't being led by their own chiefs — the kupapa often set their own limits in the wars they fought. There was also an outbreak of dysentery among the troops, including Whitmore, who had to be carried on a litter. Whitmore condemned the Arawa for their lack of action, but the truth of the matter was that the campaign was over. By 18 May the withdrawal from the Ureweras was complete.

Te Kooti had still not been caught; but for Whitmore there was a bright side. The rigours of the campaign had hardened his troops and turned them into a fighting force as good as any. Most importantly for Whitmore, however, was that Te Kooti could no longer expect to have the support of the Tuhoe. For them to do so would have spelt their extinction. Te Kooti was well aware of this and seems to have made the decision to leave before Whitmore had even entered the mountains. He headed for the Taupo region.

Te Kooti

OPEPE

The soldiers killed at Opepe were buried on the site, and the graves have been lovingly tended — in fact the last time I was there I found the withering remains of roses which had been placed at each grave not long before. Opepe is on the Napier–Taupo Road, not far from Taupo. The spot is signposted, and other signs point the way to the gravesite. I could find no trace of the village that was once there, though I have since been informed that the site is on the other side of the road, but the graves themselves, in a fenced-off area, serve as a reminder that 130-odd years is not that long ago. The gravesite is surrounded by bush and the atmosphere is quiet, yet very much alive. I found myself going a bit morbid, trying to imagine what it would be like to be so young and to die the way these men did.

When Te Kooti moved out of the Urewera mountains to the Taupo region he had about 200 followers. Of these 50 were on horseback while the rest made the trek on foot. On the way, they entered the village of Heruiwi on the edge of the ranges, where they took prisoners and all the livestock. From there they could see the light from fires in another settlement, Opepe.

The fires had been lit by a man acting as a guide for 14 volunteer cavalrymen who had arrived earlier that day, 6 June 1869. On arriving at Opepe the cavalrymen found three stray sheep which they butchered and hung up in a tree. They then settled down and waited to be joined by a group of kupapa, believing on the advice of their commanding officer Colonel St John that the camp was a safe place.

The following morning it was raining, and one of the troopers, George Crosswell, discovered that his horse had wandered during the night. He set off to look for it, but failed to find it and returned to the camp soaked to the skin. He took off his uniform and put it close to the fire to dry out, and was sitting stark naked when a small group of Maori wandered into the camp. Believing they were the kupapa reinforcements, the troopers greeted the visitors with handshakes all round; but it wasn't long before some of the troopers became suspicious. They were totally unprepared for an attack and did not have their guns with them when Te Kooti's men suddenly pounced. George Crosswell and four others made it to the safety of the surrounding bush, but the other nine men were shot and bayoneted. The killing was swift. The only man who managed to put up a fight was Sergeant-Major Slattery, a big man who grabbed a rock or a lump of wood and fought back briefly before being killed.

George Crosswell escaped into the evening and ran, walked and stumbled over 40 miles to a fort at Galatea. Considering his nakedness and the cold winter night, the escape was a remarkable one. He later stated that he was moving too fast to be bothered

Gravesite at Opepe, where Sergeant-Major Slattery and his companions are buried.

by the cold, but by the time he reached Galatea the next morning his feet had suffered terribly. Two of the others arrived at the fort over the next couple of days, and the third, Cornet Angus Smith, was found by a search party 10 days later, wandering around and in a very bad way.

The day after the attack, the bodies of the nine were found by a couple of men who were surveying the area and they passed the information to Colonel St John, who came out to Opepe with a group of Taupo Maori and buried the bodies. Te Kooti had once more proved his brilliance in the art of guerilla warfare, and had got away with horses, guns and ammunition.

After the action at Opepe, there was a lull in the fighting that was to last three months. Colonel Whitmore had gone to Auckland to recuperate from the illness he suffered during the Urewera campaign, and while he was there the government changed hands. Premier Stafford was out, and Fox was in. With Premier Fox was Donald McLean, who became the new native affairs minister. As has already been stated, Whitmore and McLean had their differences; and Whitmore's rest from military life became permanent. The new military commander was Thomas McDonnell.

Te Kooti welcomed the respite in fighting: he had some politics of his own to take care of. Leaving most of his following at Tokaanu, on the southern shores of Lake Taupo, he set off to the King Movement's capital at Tokangamutu in the King Country to convince King Tawhiao to take up the fight. He received a mixed reaction. There was no shortage of sympathy, but there appears to have been a division among the Waikato Maori as to how much support should be given and what form it should take. Associated with the King Movement and living in the King Country was a religious prophet called Hakaraia. Hakaraia had, with some success, fought his own war against the colonials and their Arawa supporters in 1867; and he and 30 of his men joined Te Kooti. It seems likely that Te Kooti was given ammunition by the Kingites, but as they were sceptical about his chances of success, they offered no direct assistance in the form of manpower. A delegation that included Rewi Maniapoto went with Te Kooti to observe the next stage of the war.

Government military operations recommenced in September 1869 with a force of between 600 and 700 men, mainly kupapa but including about 100 Europeans. On 12 September Te Kooti attacked a detachment of kupapa — about 120 Ngati Kahungunu, under the command of Henare Tomoana. Tomoana quickly entrenched and the attack was repulsed. Te Kooti lost three killed and several wounded; Ngati Kahungunu casualties were three wounded.

Te Kooti tried again at Te Ponga, and was again repulsed, with another five men dead. After these two engagements it became apparent to Rewi that Te Kooti's chances of success were slim. If he failed to beat a detachment of the forces against him, how was he to beat them *en masse*? Rewi returned to the King Country, leaving Te Kooti without Kingite support.

Te Kooti decided to fight the next phase of his war from a fixed position at Te Porere Rereao, at the edge of the bush to the northwest of Mount Tongariro. The main redoubt was roughly 20 square yards in size with flanking bastions built at opposite corners. Around the outer wall at intervals of four feet were loopholes for rifle fire, and the pa had a good escape route leading into the surrounding bush. On the outskirts of the pa were two fortified outposts. As at Ngatapa, the pa had several fatal weaknesses. The flanking bastions were poorly designed and could not protect the outside walls, and the loopholes were made with insufficient angle, so the rifles could not be fired directly into the trench that surrounded the pa. Certainly the lessons that should have been learnt at Ngatapa were not.

On the morning of 4 October McDonnell attacked with his full force. Five hundred and forty men, split into two columns, advanced on the position. The first column under the command of Major Te Kepa Te Rangihiwinui and Lt-Colonel Herrick skirmished their way up to the pa's left side, taking out the outpost and forcing a party of Ngati Tuwharetoa, who had placed themselves in an outflanking position, to retire. From there they managed to get into the trench outside the main wall, where they were joined by the second column who had advanced on the pa, clearing out the other outpost in the process. The forces found the trench to be surprisingly safe, and busied themselves with stuffing pumice into the loopholes so that the defenders could not see out, and with firing into the pa interior. As the pa was stormed many of its occupants fled into the surrounding bush. Te Kooti was surrounded by some of the women who acted as bodyguard and human shield, but in spite of this he was wounded once again, this time through the hand, losing a couple of fingers.

When the colonial troops got into the pa they shot all the males still there, as well as wounding some of the women. Thirty-seven of Te Kooti's people were killed in the battle and about 40 men, women and children were captured.

Te Kooti, who led a 'charmed life', escaped again, but this was to be his last stand from a fixed position, and from now on his fighting effectiveness was to diminish. After the battle at Te Porere he was hunted over a large part of the North Island. He first went to ground at Tuhua, and although the government learnt of this, they chose not to attack. Tuhua was inside the boundary of the King Country and the government was not prepared to do anything that might force it to fight the Waikato tribes again.

From Tuhua he went to Hakaraia's village at Tapapa, and while there he set up a meeting with an Auckland land baron, J.C. Firth. At the meeting, held at Matamata, Te Kooti said that he wanted peace and would not fight again if he was left alone. This was the same wish he had expressed upon escaping from the Chathams, and again the government rejected the offer and continued the pursuit.

With a combined force of 650 men, McDonnell closed in on Tapapa. Te Kooti moved out and McDonnell made Tapapa a base camp and sent Kepa and 200 men to tackle Te Kooti. At one point Te Kooti doubled back and attacked this force, but he lacked the numbers and couldn't press home the advantage. During the skirmishing Kepa captured 100 horses and killed four of his enemy. In the heavy fog and the confusion of the fight Te Kooti escaped in the direction of Rotorua.

It was at Rotorua that the Ringatu leader tried to make peace with the Arawa. The negotiations were about to get underway when Lt Gilbert Mair and a group of Arawa warriors came on the scene. The Arawa elders were making their way to Te Kooti when Mair threw down the white flag they were carrying and attacked. By all accounts the

Te Porere, the Outpost.

The view from Te Porere.

The main redoubt at Te Porere.

fight that followed was a determined effort on both sides. Te Kooti once more escaped, with his rear guard under Peka Makarini holding off Mair's men. He lost several more men in the battle, including Makarini, perhaps his most loyal lieutenant.

The Ringatu band made their way back to the Ureweras, but found that the place wasn't as safe as it used to be. Gilbert Mair and his 'flying column' of Arawa warriors made several expeditions into the area, trying to flush him out. There were also other forays by kupapa under the command of their own chiefs. These men were working without pay, and were hoping to catch Te Kooti and collect the 5000 pounds placed on his head.

Te Kooti's lieutenant Hakaraia was killed when, on 23 March 1870, Kepa came across a Ringatu camp and attacked. Prisoners were taken and shot, reducing Te Kooti's numbers by another 19. His followers were becoming fewer and fewer — casualties were taking their toll, and others were becoming too exhausted to continue. By the time Te Kooti left the Ureweras and made his way back to the sanctuary of the King Country, his followers consisted of five men and one woman. He remained under the protection of the Kingites and, in 1883, as part of an effort to make peace and open up the King Country, he was finally pardoned.

In 1893 Te Kooti was resting in the shade under a wagon when two fighting dogs upended it. Te Kooti received internal injuries in the accident, from which he later died.

The Ringatu faith exists to this day.

South Taranaki

While Te Kooti's war raged throughout the East Coast and Taupo regions, another even greater threat to colonial authority unfolded in South Taranaki. Te Kooti's war had terrorised and destabilised the East Coast, throwing the acquisition of land (and the power that came with it) into turmoil. At the same time the Ngati Ruanui chief and spiritual leader, Titokowaru, was waging a war that would shake the very foundations of colonial power. Te Kooti and Titokowaru did not at any stage meet and discuss joint strategy, nor had either of them been able to draw the King Movement back into the war. Had they been able to do so, there is little doubt that the end result of the New Zealand Wars would have been very different. Te Kooti certainly put the colonists in a very difficult situation; but it was Titokowaru who put them in a desperate one.

The period between the first Taranaki War and the rise of Titokowaru was not a peaceful one. It was a time when there were many battles fought over most of the region, but they were fragmented and mostly localised.

After the first Taranaki War the Maori occupied the Tataraimaka area and claimed it as theirs by right of conquest. They refused to relinquish it until the Waitara block was returned. On 11 May 1863, after a commission of inquiry found that the sale of the Waitara block was unjust, the attempted purchase was abandoned. In the weeks leading up to the return of the land, however, there was fighting in Tataraimaka and imperial troops, mainly the 57th Regiment, stormed and captured the fortified pa at Katikara.

On 30 April 1864 a large Pai Marire force attacked the redoubt at Sentry Hill. The attack was badly planned and many of the Pai Marire converts apparently believed they would be spiritually protected from the bullets fired at them. The attack was repulsed by the 57th Regiment and one estimate of casualties gave 50 killed and another 60 wounded. Among the wounded was Titokowaru, who lost the sight of one eye when a bullet grazed his face, leaving a terrible scar.

Over the next couple of years the imperial troops would gradually be withdrawn from New Zealand and replaced by colonial constabulary and militia. Wanting to make the most of the imperial troops while he still had them, Governor Grey ordered a campaign led by General Cameron to crush Maori resistance in Taranaki. Cameron was very reluctant to fight this campaign. He had come to respect his Maori adversary and was growing disillusioned about the nature of the war. There were increasing tensions between Grey and himself, which were to boil over during this operation. Cameron and a field force of about 1200 men marched from Wanganui on 24 January 1865 and headed north to Nukumaru, about 15 miles away, where they made camp.

That same day, the camp was attacked by several hundred Maori. First they fired volleys from the surrounding bush; then they came charging into the camp with guns and tomahawks, looking for targets. The fighting lasted until the following day. Although the Maori fought with obvious skill and courage, they were eventually beaten back, and about two dozen of them were killed. Cameron, who had already decided to run a slow and careful campaign, had lost 14 men, and this attack made him even more cautious.

The Maori then decided to fight Cameron from a fixed position — a pa at Weraroa. Grey put considerable pressure on Cameron to attack the pa, but Cameron, still smarting from the Waikato campaign, refused to do so. Instead he built several redoubts to protect his supply line, then secured the pa with a portion of his force and marched past it. By outflanking the pa, he deprived it of its strategic value.

Cameron then continued northwards. On reaching Te Ngaio on 13 March he came up against 200 or so members of the Ngati Ruanui. These he defeated, inflicting heavy casualties. On 31 March Cameron halted the advance, having reached the Waingongoro. It was the end of the campaign — and it was also the end of Cameron's military involvement in this country. The following August he left New Zealand.

Meanwhile Governor Grey, incensed at Cameron's refusal to attack Weraroa, mounted his own campaign against it. With colonial troops he first captured a supply depot behind the pa, then attacked the pa itself. The fight itself was a non-event, since the pa had been all but abandoned, but for Grey it proved to be a brilliant publicity stunt: after its fall he was acclaimed as a hero and a man of great military skill. There were no casualties on either side.

Cameron's replacement was Major-General Trevor Chute. Although Chute did not remain long in this country, he made a lasting impression. With an army of imperial and colonial troops and kupapa, he devastated the area from the Waitotara River to Mount Taranaki. Resistance was uncoordinated and Chute repeatedly drove out the inhabitants from unfortified villages. He burned and pillaged his way to Mt Taranaki, but the only major action was the battle of Otapawa Pa, in which 11 of his men were killed; estimates of the Maori losses are as high as 30.

Chute then made his way around Mt Taranaki, cutting a track via an inland route. On reaching New Plymouth he was hailed as a hero, although in hindsight the march had come close to being a total disaster: the army had got lost and started running out of supplies, and were forced to eat the pack horses. At least one of the men in his command had to be left behind 'with a rifle and a blanket', the men were in such a state of exhaustion. They were saved by the arrival of supplies from New Plymouth, and after nine days the ordeal was over.

The last of these Taranaki campaigns was under the command of Major Thomas McDonnell. McDonnell did not have the numbers that Chute had, but he fought along similar lines, raiding undefended villages, where the resistance was fragmented and uncoordinated.

These campaigns of McDonnell and those of Chute left a bitter legacy. There were reports of drunken soldiers burning homes and stealing whatever they could lay their hands on; and some of the raids were carried out on villages that were in the process of peace negotiations with colonial authorities.

After these raids an uneasy peace settled over southern Taranaki. During the raids many Maori fled into the interior, but to remain there would have meant starvation. Also, in the current political climate, they risked losing their land if it was not occupied. The majority of those who left soon came back and, living in the shadow of the redoubts that dotted the area, started to rebuild villages and replant crops. One of the villages that was rebuilt was Te Ngutu-o-te-Manu ('the beak of the bird').

Rebuilt in six days, Te Ngutu became the centre of Ngaruahine authority, and many meetings were held there throughout 1867 and 1868. The subject of the meetings was peace, and at the centre of the talks was the emerging Ngaruahine chief, Titokowaru.

Born into the Ngaruahine, a subtribe of Ngati Ruanui, in 1823, Titokowaru received an education from a local Brethren mission. When the Pai Marire's founder, Te Ua, died in October 1866, Titokowaru became one of the religion's leaders. In 1867 he embarked on a peace campaign that started with the meetings at Te Ngutu and continued with a series of marches, first to other villages and then to colonial centres. Titokowaru undertook these marches with an entourage of 200–300 people. He travelled the area between Taranaki and Wanganui, visiting all the subtribes of the area, convincing them of the need for peace. He declared 1867 to be 'the year of the daughters, the year of the lamb' and his visits to the subtribes and colonial garrisons eventually brought about a formal peace.

Unfortunately it was not to last. The 'fly in the ointment' was land confiscation. In 1865 the colonial government confiscated more than a million acres in Taranaki, although over half of this was later given back or bought from the legitimate owners. In South Taranaki the confiscated area was a belt of land that extended from the coast 20 miles inland, with the southern boundary at Waitotara. Some of this land was surveyed and allocated to military settlers, and some was sold off to help pay the debts of war; but the rest was left alone — the government had neither the inclination nor the resources to take possession of it. The local tribes of the area were forced to concede the area of land already taken, and were prepared to do so if it meant peace. But as peace was established and resources became available, the process of surveying and selling off land continued. This 'creeping confiscation' put the Maori population in a dilemma. They had undergone immense economic hardship as a result of Thomas McDonnell's raids on their crops and livestock, and they could not afford to lose more land. Yet past experience had taught them that it was impossible to fight the colonial army. It was in this atmosphere that Titokowaru's peace turned into Titokowaru's war.

At first, opposition was passive: survey pegs were pulled out and surveyors were told to leave. As settlers started moving into the area, they were made unwelcome, and harassed with minor thefts and the burning and pulling down of fences. This went on for about six months, but the message still wasn't getting through. In May 1868 the resident magistrate from Patea, James Booth, rode into Te Ngutu with three constables to retrieve some stolen horses and arrest the thieves. Titokowaru was ill at the time and instead Booth was received by one of his lieutenants, Toi Whakataka, who claimed that at least one of the horses was his and that he would not return the others. Booth left empty-handed and turned the matter over to McDonnell, who returned to the village with 50 or so constabulary. The inhabitants of Te Ngutu were warned of his approach, however, and those accused of the theft were able to get away. McDonnell and his men were invited in and put up for the night. In the morning they left with one of the village's spokesmen, Tauke, as 'a sort of hostage'.

It was becoming increasingly obvious to Titokowaru that hostilities would soon break out. The colonial forces at Patea numbered about 770 constabulary, with a further 150 kupapa based at Wanganui. The tribes of the area were reluctant to go to war, and Titokowaru realised that, in order to gain their support, he would have to show them that he could win. His own force consisted of no more than 80 men at this stage, so it would seem foolish for him to provoke McDonnell — yet this is exactly what he did. Titokowaru felt that his best chance was to fight McDonnell's army on ground of his choosing and at a time when McDonnell was unprepared. The place he chose was Te Ngutu.

If McDonnell was to attack, he would first have to be lured into doing so. On 9 June 1868 three European settlers were killed in a series of raids. Livestock was driven off farms, fences were pulled down, wood-chopping parties were attacked, and as settlers started to move off their farms and seek the safety of the towns and redoubts, their properties were burned and ransacked.

McDonnell was slow to react. He came under pressure to do so both from the settlers and from the government, but he wanted to train up new recruits, and — in a nutshell — he wanted to do things his own way. Further pressure came to bear when the news arrived that Te Kooti had landed at Poverty Bay. This was not a time for the army to be sitting around doing nothing.

On 2 July McDonnell was forced into action. Titokowaru had organised an attack on the redoubt at Turuturu Mokai, three miles from Waihi where the main garrison were camped in their redoubt.

TURUTURU MOKAI

Turuturu Mokai was a small redoubt, no more than 25 square yards. The walls were made of earth and fern and were five feet high on the inside; the outside of the walls led down into a surrounding ditch. The redoubt was still undergoing renovations when it was attacked: the entrance was a gap in the wall, protected by an earth shield lying across and behind it; and the loopholes in the walls for rifles had yet to be constructed. At opposite corners were flanking bastions. Since the redoubt was so close to Waihi, men on horseback could be there within 20 minutes. The site, chosen by Governor Grey in 1866, had one great weakness: it was dominated by higher ground about 150 yards away. It was this weakness that Titokowaru intended to exploit.

Titokowaru hand-picked 60 of his 80 men and instructed them on how the job was to be done. The redoubt itself was not to be stormed: instead, the attackers were to creep up to the walls under cover of darkness and make their way into the ditch. Once they were there, the defenders would have to show themselves over the top of the wall in order to fire. The idea was to draw the garrison out of the barracks and into the open where they could be picked off by sharpshooters positioned on the high ground nearby. (When I visited Turuturu Mokai I was hoping to stand on this high ground, but it is no longer there.) From a range of 150 yards and in the dim light of a new day, these sharpshooters would have had their work cut out for them. A principal concern was that the attack be carried out with minimal casualties — any reduction in numbers would be a significant loss. It would have been tempting to get into the redoubt and take more firearms, but keeping in mind that the garrison at Waihi was not far off, this was forbidden.

The attack on Turuturu Mokai was the first of several occasions on which Titokowaru proved that his talent for making peace was matched by his talent for making war.

Although he planned the attack in great detail, giving exact instructions on what to do and what not to do, Titokowaru took no part in the actual attack. The assault on Turuturu Mokai was led by two of his lieutenants, Haowhenua and Tautahi Ariki. On 11 July the war party set off to the redoubt. They spent most of the night under cover just beyond the walls, waiting for the first light of the morning.

At the time of the attack Turuturu Mokai was manned by 27 men under the command of Captain Frederick Ross, a popular officer and a close friend of McDonnell. Several people were sleeping outside the wall of the redoubt, in various outbuildings. Settler Richard Lennon spent the night in the canteen, which he owned. A couple of military settlers, Coslett Johnston and Lawrence Milmoe, were sleeping in tents. Captain Frederick Ross was on the outside too, in his own whare; and in another whare were constables Hamilton and Cowper. All these men were confident that, in the event of an attack, they could easily reach the safety of the redoubt.

At the very first light, Haowhenua and his party started creeping towards the redoubt. They had spent the cold night waiting, and the suspense, especially for the younger warriors, had been almost unbearable. As they crept forward they were spotted by the sentry, Garrett Lacey, who was shot and wounded as he raised the alarm. He found himself cut off from the redoubt and ran to the surrounding bush. Captain Ross reacted quickly, grabbing his revolver and fleeing to the redoubt dressed only in his shirt. He was joined there by Milmoe and Johnston. Cowper and Hamilton, perhaps fearing that they had been cut off, fled to the safety of the bush. Lennon decided to get fully dressed first before leaving the canteen, and the time he wasted doing this cost him his life. He finished buttoning up his tunic and lacing his boots, stepped outside and was killed at the door. Since he was the first death of the raid, his heart was cut out by the war priest and was

The Waihi fort, 20 minutes by horse from Turuturu Mokai redoubt. Taranaki Museum

scorched in accordance with an ancient tradition, while the rest of the war party made its way safely to the ditch. Inside the redoubt the men had been called to arms and they lined themselves along the walls and the flanking bastions and the fighting started in earnest. Once the defenders had been drawn outside, the marksmen who had taken up a position on the higher ground were able to take aim, and as the light became stronger they inflicted more and more casualties.

Titokowaru had made it clear that the gate to the redoubt was not to be directly attacked, but youth and enthusiasm being what it is, a group of younger warriors, and also Paipai, who was enthusiastic but not so young, charged it anyway. Captain Ross called for volunteers to defend the gate, and they managed to inflict several casualties, not without a few of their own. Constable Gaynor was killed and Peter Swords mortally wounded, and Captain Ross, who had put up a brave fight, was shot in the head. He died instantly.

Panic began to set in among some of the defenders. Five of them leapt over the walls and made a run for it. One was killed and another wounded while trying to get away, but the other three made their way to the fort at Waihi.

The sentry on guard at Waihi noticed some flashes coming from Turuturu Mokai and, thinking that it might be rifle fire, alerted the senior sergeant who in turn alerted the commanding officer — the infamous Major Gustavus Ferdinand von Tempsky.

Von Tempsky, a Polish aristocrat by birth, became a Prussian officer and had fought in the Americas before coming to New Zealand, where he spent some time goldmining in the Coromandel and as a newspaper correspondent before joining the Forest Rangers. It was while he was a captain of the Forest Rangers 2nd Division that he earned the Maori

Site of the Waihi fort today.

name Manu Rau (Many Birds) which was a reference to his ability to pop up anywhere in the course of his guerrilla campaigns.

Von Tempsky was now commanding the Constabulary No. 5 Division and had been left in charge of the Waihi fort during McDonnell's absence. He looked out towards the redoubt and saw some flashes, but as the wind was blowing in the wrong direction he could not hear any gunfire. He decided to investigate, but did so without any urgency. He proceeded to Turuturu Mokai with a detachment of constabulary on foot, leaving Waihi under the command of Major William Hunter. Senior Sergeant Anderson requested permission to saddle the horses and ready the cavalry, but Hunter was not inclined to get out of bed on this cold morning and as alarms such as these were all too frequent he refused to turn out. It was not until Lance-Corporal Cobbe, who had escaped from Turuturu Mokai, came running into Waihi and raised the alarm that Hunter reacted. He later came under severe criticism for this lack of action but, in his defence, it also seems that he was under orders from von Tempsky to stay at the camp. Von Tempsky was to gain a reputation as a bit of a glory-seeker and it's possible that, if there was a problem at Turuturu Mokai, he wanted to sort it out himself.

While von Tempsky was heading towards Turuturu Mokai he came across two more of the men who had escaped, Wilkie and Burrows, who told him that the redoubt had

The monument at Turuturu Mokai.

come under attack and that most of the men were dead. Von Tempsky took off with greater urgency, but instead of heading directly for the redoubt, he swung around to the north in an effort to intercept the raiders.

Haowhenua had sentries in place to warn of the approach of the soldiers and was amazed at the time they were taking — as were the soldiers in the redoubt. As von Tempsky approached, Titokowaru's war party gathered up their arms and six dead and headed off. Von Tempsky tried to give chase but he was too late.

Ten men died defending Turuturu Mokai and another six were wounded. When McDonnell heard the news of the death of his friend Captain Ross and the rest of the men he was furious and determined to have his revenge. He was now determined to attack Titokowaru's stronghold at Te Ngutu at the first opportunity.

Titokowaru's trap was set.

Sacred Soil

TE NGUTU-O-TE-MANU

Te Ngutu-o-te-Manu is now a park with a playground for the kids, park benches and a pleasant place to have a picnic. There is a monument dedicated to the brave men who lost their lives in the attack, though I could see no mention of those brave men who died defending it. There is also a sign that gives a brief outline of the battle there. In the wording Major von Tempsky is mentioned, but someone has crossed out the word 'Major' and replaced it with 'Mercenary'.

There are many monuments and signs around the country that give an unbalanced view of events. One of these is at the Waihi cemetery, where a monument is dedicated to the brave men who died during the capture of Te Ngutu. I have no doubt that these men were brave and should be remembered, as should all those who died fighting for their homes, their land, and their dreams, but to say that Te Ngutu was captured is, at the end of the day, going a bit far.

There were three separate attempts to capture Te Ngutu. The first attempt didn't come to much. McDonnell and 300 of his best troops marched out of Waihi on 10 August 1868 and headed for Titokowaru's capital. It rained hard and they got lost and everybody ended up going home wet and tired.

The second attempt went a little better. McDonnell decided to launch another offensive, the idea being to attack when the weather was so bad that Titokowaru would not be expecting them. He had no sooner decided on this plan than the weather turned fine and sunny and stayed that way for about a week. McDonnell gave up waiting for the rain and went to Patea to take care of some business and, of course, as soon as he got there, it came down in buckets. He raced back to Waihi and on 21 August marched out of camp with a force of 350 men.

McDonnell was right in his thinking, for when he got to Te Ngutu it was practically empty. Most of the inhabitants were away collecting food of one kind or another, with the bulk of the men out hunting wild cattle. Titokowaru and about 20 men remained in the village. After some reconnaissance McDonnell divided his force in two. Hunter, keen to regain his reputation after Turuturu Mokai, led the Wellington Rifles and No. 3 Constabulary to the right and von Tempsky took the left with Nos 2 and 5 Constabulary and the Wellington Rangers. The two columns crept forward on their bellies until they were about 100 yards from the outer earthworks of the village and then got up and charged. The few sentries managed to keep their heads long enough to fire a volley or two, inflicting wounds on a couple of the soldiers, and those inside the buildings were quick to react. Grabbing their weapons and taking up a position behind a fence, they managed to inflict more casualties before taking off into the bush. McDonnell's troops started the pursuit

Te Ngutu o te Monu.

but were called back after they reached the impenetrable bush surrounding the place. In effect McDonnell now held Te Ngutu, but he was well aware that Titokowaru's followers could return at any moment so he lost no time in ransacking the place and setting fire to as much of it as he could. Titokowaru's house was burned down, and also the great meeting house called Wharekura. Constable Burrows, who had been one of those who fled Turuturu Mokai, had volunteered to be in charge of the hand grenades, a dangerous job, and he was now given orders to toss these into as many of the buildings as he could. Not all of these bombs exploded; they were unreliable and dangerous to handle.

By now the warriors out hunting cattle had heard the gunfire and were making a hasty return to the village. McDonnell had organised a rear guard under the command of Hunter, and as they retreated, Titokowaru's men came back into their burning village.

They wanted to counter-attack immediately but Titokowaru made sure that any pursuit party would be well controlled and organised. His orders were to follow up McDonnell's men who were making their way along the muddy tracks, carrying the wounded on stretchers, but to stay under cover and fire from the safety of the bush. Titokowaru still had only a few men and could not afford to lose any.

The pursuit went as planned and more casualties were inflicted, especially as Hunter's men and those carrying the wounded made their way across the clearings in the bush. This went on for the next six miles and not until the edge of the bush was reached was the pursuit called off.

By the time McDonnell's men reached the Waingongoro River, a new problem had presented itself. The river level had risen and it was a difficult task to get the wounded and the rest of the men across.

Four of McDonnell's men were dead and eight wounded, but he had got away with valuable supplies of ammunition. It seems that Titokowaru had one casualty — the father of one of his lieutenants, Whakataka.

McDonnell immediately put together his report, which stated that the enemy was well beaten and the whole thing had been a great success. But it was not long before it was established that Titokowaru was far from being out of action, and McDonnell was once again forced to attack Te Ngutu.

On 2 September, 130 kupapa had arrived to reinforce McDonnell. Officially these men were under the command of McDonnell's brother, William, but in practice they were controlled by Kepa Te Rangihiwinui and his lieutenant Kawana Hunia. The kupapa were tough and experienced fighters and McDonnell lost no time in selecting most of these men to replace some of his more inexperienced troops. McDonnell now had at his disposal 369 men, all considered to be good quality troopers.

At Te Ngutu Titokowaru was also making arrangements for war. He had rebuilt the great meeting house, but most of the work done at the village was in preparation for another attack. Titokowaru had already moved the livestock to other locations and had crops planted in other areas, away from the village. Now that Te Ngutu was to be the centre of fighting it was important to reduce its economic value. Titokowaru had decided how he was to stage the defence. Most of the women and children had been sent away to a safer place, but the men and boys considered to be of fighting age (some as young as 12 or 13) were working furiously to have everything ready for McDonnell's attack.

McDonnell and von Tempsky were well aware that Titokowaru had his spies, so the planning of the next attack was done in the utmost secrecy. It was decided that this time they would attack the pa from the rear. In order to do this they would have to make their approach through an area called Ruaruru.

At around midnight on the morning of 7 September the officers moved quietly from tent to tent telling the men to get up and ready to move out with a minimum of noise so as not to alert Titokowaru's spies watching the camp. At about three in the morning they snuck out of Waihi and moved inland.

Their guide was Horopapera, the son of Te Atiawa war chief Hapurona, who had since ceased his war against the colonials. He led McDonnell's men through the night to the place where they thought Ruaruru was. Unfortunately the information they had was incorrect and the army was in danger of becoming lost, as they had on their first attempt. While trying to sort themselves out they suddenly heard voices. The sounds came from a small clearing that was used as a hospital, a short way to the north of Te Ngutu. McDonnell sent out scouts to investigate and when they came to the clearing they found two sick children being tended by a woman and a man who was probably Paramena, a chief of Mawhitiwhiti. The woman fled — Ngaruahine later claimed that she was hunted down and killed — and Paramena came out of one of the whare and fired his gun, taking on the whole colonial army till he was shot and killed. One of the children, a little girl, was very sick: she remained quiet and was left alone; but the other, a boy and the son of Katene, started making a noise, either out of fear or in order in raise the alarm. He was bashed to death by one of the kupapa scouts. Von Tempsky, who was there at the time, did nothing to stop the murder.

Kepa wanted to wait until the following night before attacking the village about half a mile away, but McDonnell, who wanted to avoid detection if possible, decided to attack at once. The inhabitants of Te Ngutu had heard the firing that had killed Paramena, so any possibility of surprise was lost. Titokowaru now put his plan into action.

In front of the pa was a clearing. The pa itself was surrounded by palisading, which was not as strong as it might have been. This was deliberate — Titokowaru wanted to tempt McDonnell into the clearing to make an assault on what appeared to be a weak position. On the outside of the clearing, and in the surrounding bush, were a series of rifle pits and firing positions, all camouflaged and expertly placed to enable riflemen to fire at any point in the clearing. The rifle pits were connected by covered trenches and in some cases tunnels. From these pits they could fire virtually without detection.

Titokowaru was outnumbered by eight or nine to one, but if he could make this plan work he could even up the odds. The plan was to make the clearing and the pa itself a deadly trap.

As McDonnell led his men into the clearing Titokowaru began sending out parties of warriors, under Katene, Toi, and Haowhenua, through the concealed passages and tunnels and into the rifle pits. Once there they began to fire, and it wasn't long before men began to fall. There was instant confusion — the firing seemed to be coming from all directions yet none of McDonnell's men could see their enemy. McDonnell, von Tempsky and Hunter got together and quickly held a counsel of war. They decided to go ahead and attack the pa. Kawana Hunia and his kupapa would break off to the left and in a wide outflanking move would try and attack the pa from its right. Von Tempsky would take a column and move around to the right and try to attack from there, while Hunter with McDonnell would lead another group up through the clearing.

Kawana Hunia and his men, using the cover of the bush, skirmished their way forward. They fought a cautious battle and their casualties were light in comparison to the other groups, but eventually they found themselves pinned down. Von Tempsky's men fought their way forward to a position from where he felt they could assault the pa; for the time being they were comparatively safe. It was Hunter's men who were taking the brunt of the killing.

As they were moving into their respective positions they could hear Titokowaru calling to his men outside the pa, 'Whakawhiria! (surround them!)', over and over. The soldiers fired volley after volley into the surrounding bush at an enemy they could not see, and inflicted little damage, while all the time they were falling 'like ninepins'. As men and officers fell, communication became difficult and some of the less experienced troops had a tendency to bunch up together instead of spreading out, making themselves easy targets.

Hunter's men found themselves in a position where to move forward was to lose men at an alarming rate and to stay where they were was to be picked off at leisure. It wasn't long before McDonnell realised that the situation was hopeless. He started to organise the retreat, thinking that his best option was to move off to the left where a path back to the main track appeared to be open. He sent out a couple of officers, Captains Brown and Newland, to gather up the wounded men of Hunter's and von Tempsky's columns and make their way to the track. All this took time and the retreat was a slow one. Von Tempsky received word that he was to wait until the wounded had been collected and then form a rear guard for the retreat. He was angry about this, as he felt that he was in a good position to assault the pa. He had also been lucky enough to escape Titokowaru's outflanking move and had not suffered the casualties that the other units had.

Titokowaru realised this and sent out from the pa a party of 10 men led by the Mawhitiwhiti tohunga, Wairau, who led his men to the opposite bank of the Mangotahi Stream and into a naturally concealed position. Most of von Tempsky's men were under cover but von Tempsky himself, unhappy about not being able to attack and probably cursing McDonnell, was pacing back and forth, slashing with his sword at the undergrowth, when he was shot through the head. He died instantly. The shot that killed von Tempsky was one of several fired in a volley and there were more than one who claimed to have killed him; however, a likely candidate for the honour was Te Rangihinakau, a man of considerable fighting experience, who declared he took careful aim and got him through the forehead.

A young soldier called Shanaghan tried, with the help of another, Jancey, to recover von Tempsky's body, but as they lifted him up Jancey was wounded. Shanaghan helped him to safety in the cover of the surrounding bush and then went to get help. He eventually found Lieutenant Harry Hunter, brother of Major William Hunter, and as they approached von Tempsky's body Harry was also shot dead. Shanaghan tried again, moving amongst men asking for their assistance. Nobody seemed too keen until he asked Captain Buck, who agreed to help. On this attempt Shanaghan was wounded, shot through both hands, and Buck was killed outright. Von Tempsky's body was left and was later burned by the Ngaruahine, along with the others who had died.

McDonnell in the meantime was carrying on with the retreat. Kawana Hunia was also leading his men away from the scene. They suffered few casualties; but there were still quite a few who had been left back at the clearing. Among these were four young officers, Roberts, Hirtzell, Livingston and Hastings, who took on the job of removing the rest to safety. They were fortunate to a certain extent, in that many of Titokowaru's men had gone in pursuit of McDonnell's retreating column, but the remaining men were starting to panic at the thought of being left behind, and some fled into the bush without thinking. They ended up wandering around for days, before either finding their

The death of Von Tempsky. Taranaki Museum

133

way home or being caught by the Ngaruahine and killed. Some of them never made it back, and starved to death.

One of the problems facing John Roberts and the others leading the retreat was that there were not enough men to carry out the wounded, and the dreadful decision had to be made as to whom they would save and who would be left behind. One of those left was Corporal Russell, who was left propped up against a tree with his revolver to defend himself. Legend has it that he made a good account of himself before being shot at long range. Livingston went around collecting the rifles of the dead and smashed them up so they would not fall into enemy hands. Another of the wounded, Hastings, volunteered to be one of those left behind.

Titokowaru had once again given careful instructions to the pursuit party. They were to stay under cover and harass the enemy as they retreated. The soldiers had been through all sorts of hell, and this final phase was too much for some of them. Once again they could not see the Ngaruahine on their trail, and progress though the bush was painfully slow. Panic was setting in, and many of the men started talking out loud of abandoning the wounded. It was here that Thomas McDonnell proved himself a leader. He took his turn carrying the wounded, and encouraged his men. By the end of the day his clothes had several bullet holes through them and it was a wonder he managed to escape death; but he managed to hold most of his troops together. Hunter and his men were the rear guard, and on more than one occasion the pursuing Ngaruahine cut them off from the main group. The link was restored each time, but not without casualties. Fifty-four men were needed to carry the wounded, and ammunition was starting to run out. There was no rest, and it was not until they reached the edge of the bush that the pursuing Maori from Te Ngutu turned back. The soldiers finally made it back to camp at 10 pm, and most went straight to sleep in their quarters without saying a word.

At 10 am the next day Roberts and Livingston arrived at Waihi camp. They had managed to shake off their pursuers as dusk fell, and while waiting for the moon to come up to give them enough light to find their way home, they slept. They were still very close to the pa and could hear the celebrations going on through the night. Livingston and Roberts brought out to safety 66 men including 10 wounded.

Titokowaru had repulsed the attack on Te Ngutu and inflicted at least 50 casualties — but he had achieved much more than this: in fact, he had almost totally destroyed the colonial army. After Te Ngutu the morale of the troops collapsed. Major Kemp's kupapa went home, and many of the constabulary refused to re-enlist; there were desertions and widespread drunkenness, and von Tempsky's No. 5 unit mutinied. As a result, six out of the eight European units ceased to exist. The commanders started blaming the troops, accusing them of panicking and desertion. McDonnell, who before the battle was full of praise for such units as the Wellington Rangers and the Wellington Volunteers, now called them 'drunken, useless vagabonds', among other things.

The troops, on the other hand, had a few accusations of their own. They were critical of the way some of the wounded and most of the dead were left behind, and the general feeling was that they would no more go into the field of battle with McDonnell in command. The press and the public at large blamed both officers and men. Once again the Wellington units came under severe criticism, with the press suggesting that they not be served in Wellington's public houses, and that they be shunned in general. At least one of the soldiers from these units committed suicide as a result. For Thomas McDonnell the aftermath of the battle was just as devastating as the battle itself. Before Te Ngutu he was a hero, the darling of the press, the public and his men. Now, 24 hours later, he was despised and his reputation was in tatters.

The mood at Te Ngutu, however, was a bit different from that at Waihi. The bodies of the slain colonial soldiers were laid out, stripped of clothing, jewellery and weapons, and piled up in front of Titokowaru, along with a large quantity of captured ammunition. Titokowaru, as spiritual leader, had revived certain traditional customs; and one of these was to cook one of the bodies. Not many partook of the flesh, though one who did was Katene who, by reducing to food the enemies who had killed his son, paid them the ultimate insult. Titokowaru passed out the spoils of war among his people and ordered that the bodies be taken to a separate clearing and burnt. As von Tempsky's body was placed on the fire, Titokowaru gave him this eulogy:

'In the days of the past you fought here and you fought there, and you boasted that you would always emerge safely from your battles to the bright world of life. But when you encountered me your eyes were closed in their last sleep. It could not be helped; you sought your death at my hands. And now you sleep forever.'

For Titokowaru, though, there was no time for rest. While the colonials were grappling with the concept that being European and Christian was no guarantee of military victory, he moved to Taiporohenui and set up a new base. Taiporohenui was once the headquarters of the Ngati Ruanui and was also one mile from Turuturu Mokai and within view of it. With the success of Te Ngutu he started to gain support from some of the neighbouring tribes. A contingent of Tangahoe had joined him under the leadership of Tukino and Tito Hanataua.

McDonnell, meantime, decided to have another go. The kupapa had yet to leave for Wanganui, and with a fresh division under the command of Major James Fraser and some other troops that he could still rely on, he marched out of Waihi on 20 September and, after stopping off at Turuturu Mokai to await daylight, advanced on Taiporohenui.

The colonials marched to within a couple of hundred yards and opened fire, hoping to draw out their opponents. When this bit of wishful thinking failed, they advanced further until McDonnell spotted some rifle pits and entrenchments. Thinking that he was about to walk into another trap he withdrew, and on his retreat he sent some of Fraser's men into a covered ditch to ambush any pursuit party. There was a pursuit, but as it approached the place where Fraser's men were hiding they stood up and fired — perhaps too soon — and instead of being ambushed, the pursuers were warned away. McDonnell then returned to the camp at Waihi with another disappointment. The next day the kupapa returned to Wanganui.

Throughout this time the Pakakohe (another sub-tribe of Ngati Ruanui) had remained in a state of tense neutrality. McDonnell decided to exercise his diplomacy with these people: in short, he threatened them with annihilation. The Pakakohe response was to assume that they would be blamed for any trouble within their territory, and that they may as well be guilty. They joined Titokowaru in a declaration of war that took the form of an attack on a couple of local settlers. One of these, T. Collins, was killed, and after cutting out his heart they removed his head from his body. When his remains were found, his head had been stuck on a post looking at his torso.

Now all of the subtribes of Ngati Ruanui were united. For Defence Minister Haultain this was the last straw, and McDonnell was relieved of his post as commander. As has already been stated, he was later to command troops in the war against Te Kooti at Taupo, but apart from that one last chance, his military career was over. There is some speculation as to his mental health — there is no doubt that he was a very tense man — but he was still a very competent officer, and an able and ruthless commander, and he was respected by his men. He spent much of his remaining life trying to restore his reputation; however, the stigma of Te Ngutu was to remain with him forever. Titokowaru destroyed this man, as he had destroyed von Tempsky.

Haultain ordered the remnants of the colonial army to abandon the camp at Waihi and set up a new base at Patea. For the first time the colonials had conceded territory. Farms and settlements north of Patea were abandoned and as settlers moved to the relative safety of Patea and Wanganui, the first signs of panic were starting to show.

McDonnell's replacement was Colonel George Stoddart Whitmore. Whitmore's first job was to restore discipline and then to rebuild the colonial army. He begged the government to allow him to flog his troops. One man was flogged, but the practice was seen as unsuitable and was stopped. His method of countering drunkenness was just as brutal: he closed down the pubs, keeping only the strictly regulated official canteen. He dismissed the Wellington Rifles from service, and the best men from this division were placed in the Armed Constabulary, as were all new recruits. By November the colonial army was once more an effective force.

Whitmore had an attitude problem concerning Kepa and his Wanganui contingent of kupapa: he regarded them as unreliable subordinates, when in fact they were allies. This was a distinction that caused a rift between Kepa and Whitmore; but by the time Titokowaru had moved to the new position of Moturoa, an atmosphere of cooperation developed. It was obvious that another battle was about to be fought.

MOTUROA

On 6 November 1868 Whitmore supplied his men with two days' rations and at midnight began moving his force out of Wairoa (now called Waverley) towards Moturoa. The force consisted of about 300 Europeans, and was made up of Constabulary Divisions Nos 1, 2, 3 and 6, Patea Rifles, Patea Cavalry and some of the Wairoa Militia. Initially they were joined by about 400 kupapa, but of these only about 100 under Kepa took part in the fighting. The atmosphere of cooperation between Whitmore and Mete Kingi, the leading chief of the kupapa, was still fragile, and when Whitmore started handing out orders to separate groups of kupapa, Mete objected. Mete had the support of other chiefs, and through his meddling Whitmore lost the services of 300 men. In spite of this he still believed he had sufficient men to complete the task, and decided to carry on.

Along the way they built an earthworks to act as a base for operations, and leaving their packs and other gear not needed for battle, they approached Moturoa.

Titokowaru's new camp was at the base of Okotuku Hill. The hill had once been used as a pa, but that had been destroyed by General Chute during his campaign. Instead of rebuilding the fortification there, Titokowaru decided to place his defences on the flat ground at its base. The construction consisted of a single line of palisading that stretched from a steep bush-covered gully on its right to dense bush on broken ground to its left. The palisade itself appeared to be little more that a screen, but behind it was a firing trench about six feet deep with steps cut in to enable Titokowaru's men to fire through the gap between the ground and the wall. The earth from the trench was thrown up behind, forming another firing position; and there was a third position in the form of two towers built at opposite ends of the wall and another in the middle. Although the pa gave the impression of being very easy to attack, the defenders had three lines of fire to the enemy. A clearing extended about 300 yards in front of the pa.

As Whitmore came to the edge of the clearing he drew up his assault plans. Kepa and 70 or so men made a wide outflanking move through the bush at the edge of the clearing, approaching the pa from the right (east) side. The idea was for them to get in

Moturoa Pa site. The line of defences were about 100 yards behind and running parallel to the line of cows in the foreground.

around the back of the defences and fire into them while an assault was made across the clearing to the left to tackle the palisade itself. The assault party consisted of the Patea units and the No. 3 Division under the command of Major Hunter, who was keen to avenge his brother's death at Te Ngutu and still smarting from his lack of initiative during the Turuturu Mokai affair. The rest of the men were placed at the centre of the clearing and ordered to pour as much rifle fire as possible into the palisade.

Kepa's men crept through the bush and got into position. From inside the pa not a sound could be heard, and Whitmore was convinced that he had the element of surprise on his side. This was not, however, the case — Titokowaru was well aware of their presence, and had alerted his men to take their place in the trenches and towers and to keep quiet.

Hunter's column began their advance across the clearing and got safely to within 30 yards of the pa when one shot rang out. This was soon followed by a sheet of fire, 'like hail'. Hunter's column suffered its first casualties as it took cover, and it was not long before Hunter himself was hit in the thigh, the bullet passing through an artery. As he bled to death, he passed command to Captain Newland and asked that his body be taken from the field, not left behind like his brother's.

Whitmore got up to Hunter's assault party to try and renew the effort. Once there he found men shooting wildly from behind the cover of logs and tree stumps that littered the ground. He believed that the charge could be renewed if there was some support from Kepa and from John Roberts, who was commanding the No. 6 Division, pouring in fire from the centre of the clearing.

Kepa was not having a good day either. He found the going was not as easy as he had thought. The bush was dense and impenetrable, and as he tried to move forward he came under fire from a series of rifle pits situated where he was heading. Neither Hunter nor Kepa could go any further.

At this stage Titokowaru ordered most of his men out from behind the palisade. In two prongs, leading from each side of the pa and staying under the cover of the bush, they started to encircle the clearing in a wide outflanking move, firing on Whitmore's men from very close range as they did so. Newland realised that his division was in big trouble and that help from Kepa would not be forthcoming.

Kepa had been ordered to pivot back and was able to withdraw from his position without being outflanked. Roberts was ordered to move the No. 6 Division forward and help extricate Newland's men. Roberts managed to get across the clearing with little loss after sending a detachment to help the No. 2 Division under Cumming, who was coming under fire from the bush to his left. The retreat that followed was better organised than that of Te Ngutu in that only a few isolated groups of men were left behind, and most of these managed to get themselves out, though some came within an inch of being cut off. Kepa returned to the battleground on more than one occasion to rescue wounded men in his command, but once again there were wounded from the other divisions left on the field.

Titokowaru ordered a pursuit force. Staying under cover, they remained close to the fleeing army. Most of the stretchers had been left at the earthworks along with the packs, or lost altogether, so many of the wounded were carried on rifles.

On the whole the retreat, though dangerous and unpleasant, was conducted 'by the book'. Whitmore set up a couple of groups to act as the rear guard, with each group supporting the other, and once clear of the bush his force headed across the more open ground back to Wairoa. Titokowaru's men stayed at the edge of the bush and fired volleys that inflicted a few more casualties. Three European soldiers were shot as they moved across the open ground from a range of 500 yards.

Through that night the 800 or so troops crammed into a redoubt built to hold 100 had a sleepless night, with Titokowaru's warriors firing volleys at them from long range on several occasions. The next day Whitmore left the Wairoa Rifles, about 100 men, to garrison the Wairoa settlement, and moved the rest of his force to Patea. Like McDonnell before him, it was now his turn to write a difficult report. The European troops and Kepa received praise for the way in which they conducted themselves during the battle, but the blame for the defeat was heaped upon the kupapa who had refused to take part. He accused them of 'cowardice' — something that no doubt did little to restore his relationship with an important ally. The report also understated the casualties by about half, and in a private letter that accompanied the report he poured scorn on some of his officers including, oddly enough, Roberts, whose cool thinking had been instrumental in saving Hunter's column from probable annihilation.

Whitmore felt that without massive reinforcements he could do little more than protect Wanganui and its immediate surrounding area. As such he left Fraser's division to look after Patea and withdrew with about 250 men to Nukumaru, where he entrenched.

Titokowaru stayed at Moturoa for four days, resting, recuperating and celebrating another victory. During this time another corpse was cooked. Titokowaru once again refused to eat any of it; the only ones who did were some of the new recruits, who did so as some kind of initiation.

Titokowaru lost no time in pushing home his latest victory. He moved his force to Papatupu to occupy the land left by the retreating settlers, and also to drum up more support. Some of the chiefs were reluctant to join him, but many of their followers, especially the younger warriors, were happy to enter into the fight. Support came from all over the Taranaki area and before long Titokowaru had about 1000 people, including 400 armed warriors. With what could now be described as an army, he moved again, this time to Nukumaru, about a mile from Whitmore's position.

As the news of the defeat at Moturoa spread throughout the colony, people started to panic. Haultain sent out orders to his recruitment officers to redouble their efforts, and one of them, Captain Stack, was sent to Melbourne to buy guns and to recruit 200 men. As an incentive, he was to be paid one pound for each man he brought back.

Some of the wealthy Wanganui inhabitants left the country, while others fortified their farm buildings. Those who did not have the resources to do either abandoned their farms and flooded into Wanganui which, like New Plymouth in 1861, became a town under siege. To make matters worse, the news arrived of Te Kooti's raid on Poverty Bay, and this added terror to an already tense situation.

Whitmore's plan was to tackle Te Kooti first: leaving Wanganui to be defended by the constant flow of new troops, he would take the best men with him to the East Coast, finish Te Kooti off and return to deal with the bigger and more serious problem, Titokowaru. When the citizens of Wanganui learnt of this they were not at all enthusiastic. Whitmore had never been a contender for 'most-loved citizen', and now placards that read 'No Whitmore' began appearing on the streets.

Before leaving he 'battened down the hatches' — he abandoned his position at Nukumaru and set up another at Kai Iwi, only about nine miles from Wanganui. He cleared out the garrison at Weraroa which had recently come under attack from Titokowaru, and evacuated all women and children as well as government stores from Patea.

Whitmore had other business to attend to as well. No word had been received from the garrison at Wairoa for over two weeks, and in order to find out whether they were dead or alive Whitmore sent out 66 men of the Kai Iwi Cavalry under the command of Captain Newland. With Newland were Lieutenant John Bryce — a man who was later to do well as a politician and who will resurface in this story — and Sergeant George Maxwell.

The cavalry left the Woodall redoubt at Kai Iwi and made their way to Wairoa. There they found the garrison in one piece and in high spirits. The cavalry stayed the night and helped to lower the supply of spirits before setting off the next morning back to Kai Iwi. On the way they made a stop at Titokowaru's new camp at Nukumaru. Newland, hoping to score a few merit points with Whitmore, had requested permission to do this, and Whitmore had agreed.

They changed direction, heading inland to Titokowaru's pa, and while crossing Handley's farm they stopped and crept forward to observe the goings on. At the time the pa was far from completed, and the work had stopped for the day and a celebration was taking place. A new contingent of Ngarauru had arrived and a feast was being prepared.

Newland and Bryce had gained what information they could, which was very little, and were moving off when in the distance they heard a pig squealing. A group of a dozen children, the oldest of whom was about 10, had come down from the pa and onto Handley's abandoned farm. They had found a pig and were in the process of trying to

Kai Iwi Cavalry. Taranaki Museum.

kill the poor animal with their pocket knives when they were spotted from a distance by the cavalry. From that distance, the age of the people in the group could not be determined, but it was clear that they were Maori from the pa.

Newland ordered a volley to be fired — a mistake, as it was heard from the pa — and before any further orders could be given, groups of the cavalry broke away and charged the 500 yards toward the figures below. As they drew closer it must have become obvious that the Maori were unarmed and that they were only children, but in spite of this the chase continued. One group rode straight into a swamp and got themselves stuck, but another group with Sergeant Maxwell in the lead soon found themselves on the heels of the fleeing children. Before this stupidity was over six of the children had been shot or slashed at with sabres while running as fast as they could in the direction of the pa. Two of them were killed.

The firing was heard from the pa and the parents of the children quickly realised the situation. Within seconds armed warriors poured out of the pa, two miles away, and ran towards the direction the firing had come from.

Most of the cavalry had remained at the woolshed where the pig had been found, but eventually John Bryce managed to get in front of Maxwell and ordered him to back off. Bryce was well aware that the pa had probably been alerted and saw the need to get his small force away. At first Maxwell refused to cooperate and was so excited that he wanted to take the whole of Titokowaru's force on. Indeed when Bryce rode up, the five cavalry men, Maxwell, Wicksteed, Peake, Wright and Campbell were comparing scores and readying themselves to renew the charge. The Maori from the pa were closing in and were almost within rifle range before Bryce could convince the men to help extract those stuck in the swamp. They got away only just in time.

It's easy to feel self-righteous when talking about innocent people being killed during war — in this case, very easy. But the killings at Handley's farm were done for no reason — it was sport. To make matters worse, when the cavalry got back to Kai Iwi the incident was described as a successful engagement with the enemy and Maxwell was praised for his 'extreme gallantry'. Eventually rumours began to circulate that contained elements of the truth, but by then the public had other things to worry about.

Stationed at Wanganui during its hour of need were the last of the imperial troops. The 18th Regiment were awaiting withdrawal, and in the meantime were under strict instructions to act solely as a defensive force — they were not to set foot outside the town of Wanganui. Governor Bowen had made several requests to the 'homeland' for imperial troops to be sent to New Zealand, but these requests were denied. The British government had already spent millions of pounds defending the colony, and in spite of many arguments, the New Zealand government had failed to meet any of the costs. In effect the mother country had pushed its fledgling colony out of the nest. New Zealand was on its own.

Another problem for the colonial government was the possible intervention of the Kingite tribes from the Waikato. Titokowaru realised that if the Waikato tribes re-entered the war the colonials would be fighting on the east coast, the west coast and on another front against the King Movement. Titokowaru had burnt a few bridges with the Kingites during his peace campaign when he rejected the King Movement and refused to acknowledge the authority of King Tawhiao. This was something that would not be forgotten quickly; but after Titokowaru had scored successive victories in South Taranaki, some factions within the King Movement were starting to talk once more of war.

Two of those who saw it as an opportunity too good to miss were the Kingite chiefs Tikaokao and Reihana. They proposed a small-scale raid in northern Taranaki.

PUKEARUHE

On 13 February 1869 a Maniapoto war party of 15 armed men commanded by Hone Wetere Te Rerenga raided an outpost that was lightly manned by military settlers. This taua, accompanied by another four people who were trading in the area and who were taken as interpreters, approached the redoubt at Pukearuhe in North Taranaki, overlooking the Whitecliffs area. Leaving their guns aside they spoke to two men inside, saying that they had some pigs and peaches they were willing to trade. These two men, John Milne and Edward Richards, followed Hone Wetere and some of his party to the beach where they were quickly dispatched with a taiaha. Next the taua went to the home of Bamber Gascoigne and family.

Arriving at the house they found it empty — the family had gone for a summer's day walk — so they went into the house and removed the Gascoignes' guns and waited outside. When Gascoigne and his wife Annie and their three children, one a baby and the others aged three and five, came back to the house they found themselves confronted by the armed party. Gascoigne made a dash for the house, probably to retrieve his weapons, and as he reached the porch he was killed with two blows to the back of the head with a taiaha and further blows with an axe that lay nearby. He had been carrying the baby, and she too was killed, with a blow from a tomahawk. Annie Gascoigne grabbed the remaining two children and ran for the redoubt. They were pursued by members of the taua and killed. Annie had shown some signs of putting up a fight to save the lives of herself and her children. The Gascoignes' dog and two cats were also killed and as the taua was sitting outside the house eating the food that they found there, the missionary John Whiteley

Pukearuhe in the 1860s. Taranaki Museum

John Whiteley's memorial, Pukearuhe, marks the spot where he was killed.

approached. He had come to Pukearuhe to deliver the church service the next day.

The first shot killed Whiteley's horse, and fearing the worst, the missionary got on his knees and prayed. While doing so he was shot five times with an Enfield rifle, presumably taken from the Gascoigne household.

There is a possibility that the raid on Pukearuhe was ordered by King Tawhiao himself, although when he heard of the killing of the woman and children he is reported to have said, 'This is not my work.'

Pukearuhe is on the coast, a little to the north of Urenui, and from there, there is a beautiful view of the Whitecliffs area with its rugged North Taranaki coastline. I checked out the monument to John Whiteley, erected on the spot where he died, and then made my way down to the beach. I suspect the coast has undergone little change since the events that plunged it into history; and it dawned on me that I was probably in the same area where the Gascoignes had enjoyed their last summer walk together, 130 years ago. I couldn't help but feel sorry for Annie Gascoigne, as I imagined what it must have been like for her, witnessing the killing of her husband and baby, and attempting to save the lives of her other children.

The journals of John Whiteley are in the archives of the Auckland War Memorial Museum, and they make interesting reading. He made it clear to his Maori parishioners that to take up arms against the Pakeha was a sin against God, and that he himself would take a dim view of it. The poor man's arrival at Pukearuhe was definitely a case of being in the wrong place at the wrong time; but my sympathy for him was mixed with a little scepticism, as it has been suggested that he also acted as a spy for the colonials . . .

In the days leading up to the raid on Pukearuhe, events were unfolding at Nukumaru that would change the course of the war.

If ever there were a prize to be handed out for the best pa, no doubt the competition would be stiff. Kawiti's pa at Ohaeawai and Ruapekapeka would have to be contenders, as would Gate Pa at Tauranga, and the architects at Paterangi would win at least a consolation prize for effort. But if I were a betting man, my money would go to Titokowaru and the pa Tauranga-ika.

Looking over the basic plans of this pa would be enough to get designers' hearts beating. The pa was in the shape of a diamond with slightly concave walls, and at each corner was a low tower built as a firing position, to protect the outer walls from assault. The walls consisted of two lines of palisades made from heavy trunks sunk deep in the ground, with lighter timber in between. There was a gap of about a foot and a half between the ground and the base of the walls for the riflemen to fire through from the trench that completely surrounded the inside of the pa. The trench was covered with a roof that acted as another position for a second line of riflemen who fired between gaps in the walls. The interior of the pa was dotted with artillery bunkers to keep the inhabitants safe during shelling. These bombproof bunkers were small and numerous, so that if any received a direct hit the damage and casualties would be limited to that one bunker. The roofs were made of iron and other materials taken from nearby farms which had been abandoned, and were protected by layers of earth and fern to absorb the shock. Tunnels from the bunkers to the trench ensured that the warriors could move about the interior in safety. Three sides of the pa were within close range of dense bush that made close reconnaissance impossible, and within the bush were hidden rifle pits that could be used to outflank any unlikely assaults from those directions. In short the pa was most probably unassailable.

Titokowaru had gained many more supporters since his victories at Te Ngutu and Moturoa, but he was still heavily outnumbered; and whereas before he used his genius to set traps and outmanœuvre his enemies, this time it appeared that his next victory would be more conventional. No traps, just a brilliant piece of engineering.

During the construction of the pa, Whitmore sent out patrols to gain what information he could. The second of these took place on 27 December 1868 and consisted of 10 men including Sergeant Maxwell. As they approached the pa, all seemed quiet, and to make sure that no one was home, the patrol fired shots into the pa. This was a trap, for shots were returned with great gusto and several horses were hit. One of the cavalry, Henry Wright, was trapped under his horse and no one was keen to help him until his brother, Arthur came to his rescue. It was only after Arthur accused his comrades of cowardice that some returned, and while they were getting Henry free, shots were fired at one of Titokowaru's lieutenants, Kereopa, who had come out of the pa with his tomahawk to deal to Henry. Kereopa was wounded, apparently shot in the buttocks, and the cavalry escaped. It seemed that they had all gotten away — until Maxwell, who had just ridden 150 yards, slid silently from his horse and landed dead on the ground, not far from where he had terrorised and killed those children a month before.

Colonel Whitmore now had more than 1000 men under his command. While some of these were undergoing training, others were out building and repairing the road and bridges to carry the army to Tauranga-ika. On 2 February 1869 Whitmore had amassed his troops before Tauranga-ika, where he took up the centre and his second-in-command, Lt-Colonel Lyon, moved up on the right. The troops entrenched themselves as they moved forward. It was slow work, but it was necessary to protect the troops from the constant firing coming from the pa. Whitmore had managed to get his men to within 200 yards of the pa and Lyon to within 100 yards. Lyon's men were close enough to converse with the Maori in the pa, and some of the conversation verged on the jovial — though some of it was also fairly impolite. One of the garrison within the pa suggested that they send up the fat ones first so that they could be cooked and eaten.

Whitmore had with him several Cohorn mortars which could fire an eight-and-a-half pound shell, and two six-pound Armstrong guns. These opened fire late in the afternoon, though with little effect, and the troops settled down for the night, 'singing camp songs', to the encouragement of the Maori in the pa.

Whitmore intended to charge the pa in the morning, but as the sun came up there was silence from within the walls. Many of the troops thought it was a trap — a reasonable conclusion, considering the events of Te Ngutu and Moturoa — but eventually Solomon Black, Ben Biddle and another constable walked straight up to the pa, climbed over the walls and had a look. The place was deserted with the exception of one small puppy that had been left behind.

The full extent of the mystery surrounding events at Tauranga-ika is a story that has yet to be told. Whitmore initially claimed that they had left because they were afraid of the assault planned for the next day, though he later said, after having inspected the pa, that the place was unassailable. Other explanations such as the shortage of food or ammunition don't hold up to close scrutiny.

One of the pa's inhabitants was a man who had deserted the imperial army and had

The hill behind the church is said to be the site of Tauranga-ika.

come to live with Titokowaru and his followers. He was Kimble Bent, described as a mild-mannered man who found that he was not made of the right stuff to be a soldier. When he deserted he was found and taken in by Titokowaru, and his skill at repairing guns and making ammunition were sufficient to make him a useful addition to the tribe. To all accounts he was a remarkable man and his story is a fascinating one. His interviews with the historian James Cowan give an interesting insight into the wars of this country. Of Tauranga-ika, Bent claims that the reason for the abandonment of the pa was not the lack of food, ammunition or courage, but an act of infidelity.

Titokowaru was detected in a sexual liaison, the details of which have yet to surface, but it was serious enough for him to lose his mana tapu — his sacred authority. When the act was discovered, a meeting was held, and it was decided that the fight could no longer be continued with Titokowaru in charge. Tauranga-ika was silently abandoned in the night and Titokowaru's war was effectively over. All sorts of speculation surrounds this event, including a theory that the act was a deliberate way for Titokowaru to call a halt to the war. No doubt someone knows the truth of the matter, and maybe there will be a time when the full story is told.

The evacuation of Tauranga-ika did little to ease the minds of the colonists. Titokowaru had lost much of his support, but the colonials, at this stage, were not aware of this. Within 10 days of the evacuation of the pa came the news of the raid at Pukearuhe, and it was news that sent a shiver down many spines. It now appeared that the Waikato tribes were going to enter the war. This fear was partly confirmed by the presence of 600 men, under the Waikato chiefs Tikaokao and Reihana, at the mouth of the Mokau River in North Taranaki. The intention of these warriors was unclear: they could have been there to meet any retaliation from the Pukearuhe raid; or they could have been planning to invade New Plymouth, thus opening up another front; or they might be meeting up with Titokowaru's forces. All of these options were unpleasant for the colonials to contemplate.

On learning of the evacuation of Tauranga-ika, Whitmore set off in pursuit with the fastest-moving troops he could muster. These included the newly formed No. 8 Division made up of Arawa tribesmen, and Kepa's Wanganui kupapa and the volunteer cavalry supported by No. 3 and No. 6 Divisions of constabulary. Titokowaru was fast losing support, but this did not mean that he couldn't fight. The first encounter was at Weraroa where, with a rear guard of only 40 or so, he managed to fight off Whitmore's 700 troops long enough to make his escape.

From there he made his way to an area called Oteka. Oteka was inland, about seven miles from Weraroa, set in the bush in the middle of very difficult terrain. Whitmore sent out scouting parties to find him, but many of his troops were reluctant to enter the dense bush. His troops found the hunting of Titokowaru a very tense business, and motivation was not as strong as it could have been. To counter this Whitmore introduced various methods to inspire his men. He successfully reintroduced the lash — cowardice and desertion meant 50 lashes and two years' hard labour. He also announced more 'positive' measures. Any enemy women caught were handed over to the troops and in effect became involuntary sexual partners. This practice was also used during the East Coast campaign and was endorsed by the government of the time. That such behaviour existed, at a time when there was a campaign to convert Maori to 'civilisation' and 'Christianity', defies reason.

Another dubious inducement was a bounty paid to any who brought in 'rebels', dead or alive. The price was five pounds for a warrior, 10 pounds for a chief and 1000 pounds for Titokowaru himself. Titokowaru responded by offering two shillings and sixpence for the head of Governor Bowen. The price of five pounds per head was taken literally on more than one occasion: Pakeha and kupapa soldiers went around collecting the heads of their enemies, and on at least one occasion a sack of heads was emptied out in front of Whitmore — one of which rolled under his bed. It's been said that Whitmore was shocked, but nevertheless he still paid up. On another occasion, during the chase of Titokowaru's followers, some children, their mothers and a Ngaruahine chief had lagged behind, due to the physical exhaustion suffered by the children especially, and had become separated from the main body. They were caught by some of Kepa's vanguard consisting of Wanganui and Arawa kupapa and the Pakeha Tom Adamson. The Ngaruanui chief broke away from the party to draw the vanguard away from the children, but without ammunition he could not put up much of a fight. He was caught and a fight broke out as to who was to have the head. Adamson won and took his trophy. It was not determined what happened to the children, though it is perhaps worth mentioning that, once the heads were smoked and dried, it was very difficult to judge the sex or age of the victims.

Titokowaru had no time to linger, and it was not long before he was on the move again. All the time his support became less and less and his people suffered terribly during the forced marches through extremely difficult terrain, with Whitmore's forces never far behind. In spite of his difficulties he continued to evade capture and managed to keep his people together. Eventually he made his way to the village of Otautu where he rested with his followers for a couple of days. Whitmore learnt of his presence there and on the morning of 12 March he and his men crept up through the heavy fog to within striking distance of the village. They got so close that they could have reached out and touched some of the sentries patrolling the bush. One of the sentries, Te Wareo, suddenly realised what was going on and fired his pistol to raise the alarm. Titokowaru's people fled the village and, following a predetermined plan, made their way down to the river. The crossing had to be made by canoe, and it took a couple of hours to get everybody to the other side. In the meantime Titokowaru's warriors had positioned themselves just under the lip of a ravine and from there held up Whitmore's forces. Under cover and in a position that could not be seen through the fog, they poured fire on Whitmore's advancing troops, forcing them to take cover. One of Titokowaru's men, Hakopa Te Matauawa was not at the ravine. He was dressed in the clothing of the constabulary, taken in a previous battle, and he took up a position at the end of the line of constabulary, obscured by the fog. From there he shouted out impossible and confusing instructions to the constabulary and shot the occasional straggler as the opportunity arose.

Titokowaru kept the colonials and kupapa back long enough for his people to escape and then withdrew his rear guard and escaped into the bush. Whitmore was keen to continue the pursuit but as the soldiers poured into the village they became more interested in the plunder they found.

Titokowaru had escaped once again, but in the rush to get away they were forced to abandon supplies of food, clothing and blankets, and most of their ammunition.

Without the ammunition Titokowaru ceased to be a fighting force, and as he made his way to Te Ngaere the suffering of his followers was greatly increased. The terrain became virtually impossible and exhaustion and illness were taking their toll. As people died they were buried or hidden as well as possible. The skeleton of one was later found, upright in a hollow tree. The sick and wounded were carried on makeshift stretchers and for the old and the very young life turned into a nightmare.

Te Ngaere was a series of villages built on solid ground but surrounded by vast areas of swamp, close to the track that General Chute had used on his 'conquest' march around Mount Taranaki. It was inhabited by the Ngati Tupaea, and they took Titokowaru and his people in, though some were reluctant.

For Whitmore the going also got tough. Fever and dysentery had broken out among his men and, in spite of the threat of the lash and the rewards offered, many were still unenthusiastic. He came to the edge of the Te Ngaere swamp on 23 March and was still determined to capture the Hau Hau leader. For the next two days his men were busy making fascines to lay across the swamp, and once they were ready they closed in. It was here that Whitmore was to be foiled by some tribal politics. The Wanganui kupapa were related to Ngati Tupaea and were loath to fire on them; so when Whitmore came across the village he found that the Wanganui kupapa had got there before him. The Ngati Tupaea had surrendered to them and were standing between Whitmore's troops and the fleeing remnants of Titokowaru's people.

From Te Ngaere, Titokowaru went to Kawau on the banks of the Waitara River, and there he remained for some time. Whitmore had received reinforcements — some Ngati Porou and even some Ngapuhi from Northland — but it was too late. The Arawa were not keen to start a war that might bring down the wrath of the Waikato tribes, who still had 600 men at the mouth of the Mokau River; and a new war in North Taranaki was something the colonials wanted to avoid. The kupapa withdrew, and without them Whitmore's force shrank to 400 men. In the end it was thought best, while Titokowaru was not waging war, to leave him in peace.

Whitmore returned to the East Coast and his fight with Te Kooti, robbed of his revenge against Titokowaru. The Waikato warriors, massed at the mouth of the Mokau River, realised that Titokowaru was a spent force and withdrew. For Titokowaru, his war was over: he had not won it, but neither had Whitmore. In war there are no prizes for 'just about winning' — but I can't help but wonder what sort of country this would be today if the Kingites had joined forces with Titokowaru.

PARIHAKA

Titokowaru remained at Kawau on the banks of the Waitara River. He had fortified the pa and his following had increased to about 300 people. More importantly, he had undergone a series of rituals that had absolved him of his sin. Among the military officers stationed in Taranaki were those, including Whitmore, who wanted to launch another campaign against him, but the threat of a new war that would have involved the North Taranaki tribes and possibly the King Movement was seen by the government as too big a risk.

Titokowaru had at one stage also wanted to renew the war, but he was talked out of this by the war chief turned peacemaker Hapurona. In 1871 Titokowaru returned to South Taranaki with his following and took up residence at Okaiawa. Once there, his mood changed. He resolved to wage war no more; instead, he once again preached the virtues of peace.

Throughout the 1870s South Taranaki existed as a kind of independent state. The land between the Stoney River in the north and the Waingongoro River in the south was still nominally confiscated, but the government realised that to take actual possession would be to restart the war; and the memory of the defeats at Te Ngutu and Moturoa were sufficient to persuade them against this. From this point of view Titokowaru had, in fact, won the war.

The new capital of the independent state of South Taranaki was Parihaka. This was a big village with a population measuring in the hundreds. The leadership was divided between the two prophets, Te Whiti o Rongomai and Tohu Kakahi. Te Whiti and Tohu

Parikaha as Titokowaru would have known it. Taranaki Museum.

became the voice of a people who were emerging from war to an uncertain future, and their policy of peace, preached constantly at huge meetings held at Parihaka, was to hold the population together. Titokowaru allied himself with Te Whiti and Tohu, and under their combined leadership the area and the people living in it thrived, both socially and economically.

In 1879, however, the government stepped in and once again started to survey the 'confiscated' area. Te Whiti and Tohu met this new threat with passive resistance. Initially the government handled the affair with kid gloves: the influential chiefs of the area and their families were invited to government meetings where they were fed fancy food and given lavish gifts — silks, sidesaddles, nights at the theatre and so on. Secret payments of money were also made, in an effort to bring about an acceptance of government policy. Titokowaru accepted some of this money, but passed it on to the village of Parihaka and continued to oppose the surveying.

Te Whiti and Tohu wanted to know just what the government policy was — but found it hard to get a clear answer. They had been told that areas of land would be set aside as Maori reserves, but just how much land and its location had not been decided.

While the leaders at Parihaka were trying to sort out their intentions, the government was advertising, as far away as Melbourne, the sale of land in Taranaki.

The surveying continued and the building of a coastal road from the Stoney River to the Waingongoro River was started. Te Whiti and Tohu stated their objections, but with little effect, so they went one step further. They sent out parties of men to plough through the survey lines and construct fences across the affected areas. The government response was to arrest and imprison the ploughmen. As they were arrested they were replaced with others: this continued until there were hundreds of arrests. When a fence was torn down it was quickly rebuilt, and Te Whiti, who told the government that it was he who ordered the land to be ploughed, also said that when there were no more men left he would send out the women and children.

The arrests were orchestrated by John Bryce. He had risen from being an officer in the Kai Iwi Cavalry and was now the native minister, but in spite of his promotion he was still unable to open up South Taranaki.

The Maori at Parihaka were gaining widespread support from all over New Zealand, as well as from Britain itself. There were protests at the imprisonment of Te Whiti's ploughmen, and questions were raised as to the legality of the situation. The government was getting nowhere and the process was costing them 5000 pounds per month.

Current-day Parihaka.

Eventually the surveying was stopped, and early in 1881 Bryce resigned. By October the same year, though, he was back in power, and this time he took another initiative — he invaded Parihaka.

On 5 November 1881 John Bryce and over 1600 armed constabulary and volunteers marched into Parihaka. Te Whiti and Tohu had given strict instructions that they were not to be violently resisted, and when the troops marched in they were met by lines of singing children, some of whom were holding skipping ropes across the path of the advancing soldiers.

Bryce was to come in for some severe criticism for the amount of force he used to crush a peaceful people; but he had memories of the war with Titokowaru and was probably not inclined to take any chances. Te Whiti, Tohu and Titokowaru offered themselves for arrest and were taken away. The inhabitants of Parihaka were cleared out of the way and the village was destroyed. Titokowaru spent eight months in the New Plymouth gaol before appearing in court. The charges were rubbished by the judge and he was released. Te Whiti and Tohu were held for two years at different places and never had charges brought against them. Eventually they were released and they returned to Parihaka. The village was rebuilt and remained the cultural centre of coastal Taranaki, as it still is today.

Titokowaru spent the rest of his life preaching peace. He was arrested again on a charge of 'malicious trespass' and spent another month in a Wellington gaol. Much weakened by pneumonia and asthma, Titokowaru, the greatest of New Zealand's generals, died on 18 August 1888.

I found Parihaka Road on the map and had no idea what was there. As I drove closer I felt a sense of anticipation creeping over me. I tried to dismiss it, and failed to do so. A signpost with the words 'Parihaka Pa' directed me up a long driveway past a cemetery, up to the gate. I stopped and got out of my car, surprised to find myself looking at a village that was very much a going concern. Looking out over the village I could see houses, big and small, dotted throughout the area. I discovered that I was both nervous and excited.

Throughout the course of my travels I had been in some very special places; but in arriving at Parihaka I felt as though I had reached my Mecca. I also felt that I didn't belong here — that I was trespassing — and there was no way that I was going to take photographs without first finding someone to talk to.

The pa appeared to be deserted — there was not a soul anywhere — but I had the distinct impression that there were in fact many people here, and what's more, they knew of my presence. I was looking for any sign of life, someone who could at least point me in the right direction, even if that direction was the exit: at least then I would know for sure. I stood there for a couple of minutes, not sure of which house to approach, when I noticed that a clothesline that was empty a minute ago now had white sheets hanging off it, flapping in the light breeze. Seeing the white cloth I thought, 'I surrender'; and I went around the back of the house, knowing at least that someone was home. The door was open and I knocked and poked my head inside, and there sitting at a sewing machine was Ngaio Tairawhiti. Ngaio looked at me with a quizzical expression, but she was obviously a friendly sort and I felt instantly much more at ease.

I started my 'Hi, I'm Neil Finlay and I'm putting together material for this book . . .' routine, and Ngaio listened patiently. We chatted about this and that and I told her of my impressions on arriving here. She laughed and said, 'Did you now?', in a knowing sort of way. She said that it would be fine to take photos but would I mind coming back and doing so after her husband had returned at about four o'clock. No problem. I shot off, first to Te Ngutu and then to Turuturu Mokai — two places I really wanted to see. All in all it was a very good day.

I returned to Parihaka and met Ngaio's husband Jim, who confirmed that it was all right to take photos, and pointed out where I could go — and where, perhaps, it would be best not to go. I grabbed a camera and went exploring, all the time being aware of people but not seeing anyone. I went back to Ngaio and Jim's house and found a cup of tea and a piece of apple pie waiting for me.

Back in the 1870s King Tawhiao had sent 12 disciples to Parihaka, and Jim, who was the kaitiaki (manager) of the pa, was a descendant of one of these. He filled me in on some of the history of the place — but it was a story that would take more time than either of us had at that moment. One day I hope it will be told.

By the time I had finished taking the photographs I was exhausted from all the travelling and the events of the day. Thanks to the warmth and generosity of Jim and Ngaio, when I left Parihaka I felt as if I had been fully recharged. Some people are like that.

Bastion Point

By May 1872 the last angry shots of the New Zealand Wars had been fired and the fighting had at last died down. The results, though, were inconclusive. The King Movement was still very much intact and its army was strong enough to continue the fight, should the colonial government be tempted to do so. It wasn't. Te Kooti had not been caught and although Titokowaru could possibly have united the tribes of North and South Taranaki and continued his war, he chose instead to live a peaceful life. A truce, though an uneasy one at times, prevailed.

The process of land acquisition, however, continued. Instead of using the gun the government found a new and more effective method, the law. As has already been discussed, the Native Land Acts of 1862 and 1865 allowed for tribal lands to be split up into titles awarded to individuals upon application to the land courts. Once a title had been granted the process of buying the land became an easy one. Areas of land set aside as reserves to enable Maori to establish some sort of economic base came under the administration of government officials, and much of the land was offered for lease to Pakeha settlers. The financial return of the leases was more often than not minimal; in many cases it was less than what was being received as rates by the local councils.

During the 1860s when these laws first came into effect, there was no Maori representation in the New Zealand government and it was not until well after the turn of the century that voices fighting for the rights of Maori would be heard.

The story of Bastion Point is a good example of how the land laws were used in the process of Maori land alienation.

As the city of Auckland grew the pressure put on Ngati Whatua Maori to sell more land increased. In an effort to protect at least some of the land for future generations the Ngati Whatua chief Te Kawau applied to the land court for a title to 280 hectares of land at Orakei. The title was issued with a clause that stated that 'the land shall be totally inalienable'. The title included the names of 13 members of Ngati Whatua as

Bastion Point.

the landowners, thus from a legal point of view, dispossessing all other tribal members of their interests in the land. From the word go, the issue of ownership became confused, and the laws passed down from on high were insufficient to deal with tribal lands.

In spite of the 'inalienable' clause the land at Bastion Point would fall, bit by bit, into government hands. In 1882 the Orakei Native Reserve Act allowed for the land to be leased for periods of up to 42 years, and in 1898 the land court partitioned the land into titles belonging to the 13 people named on the original title, or their descendants, giving them the right to sell. In the period between 1910 and 1914 a sewage system was built that polluted the shellfish beds surrounding the point, and when the road was built it covered the stormwater drain, turning areas of land into swamp during the winter.

The government had ensured, by Orders in Council, that land speculators were excluded from buying land at Bastion Point, and by 1928 the Crown had purchased all but 1.2 hectares. The buying of the land was a messy and complicated affair, and one that was resisted by Ngati Whatua living on the land. Ngati Whatua organised 15 parliamentary petitions, and there were 16 different actions in the land courts, the supreme court and the court of appeal as well as six appearances before commissions or committees of inquiry, but to no avail.

The land that was to remain in Maori ownership for the generations to come was now in the hands of the Crown, and in 1951 the people living on Bastion Point were evicted and moved into state houses built adjacent to the land in Kitemoana Street. The inhabitants, one of whom was a small boy called Joseph Parata Hawke, watched as their homes were burnt to the ground. Joe Hawke became involved in cultural politics during the 1970s, and in 1977, when the government announced plans to subdivide Bastion Point, he led the Orakei Maori Action Group and 150 protesters back onto the land and demanded its return. Caravans and tents were set up along with cooking facilities and a meeting house which became the home of the protesters for the next 506 days.

During the occupation Ngati Whatua elders entered negotiations with the government and a deal was struck whereby the government would return a total of 11.2 hectares, and the inhabitants of the state houses in Kitemoana Street could buy the freehold title on those properties for $275,000. Joe Hawke turned the offer down, and finally on 25 May 1978, 600 police moved onto the point. They cleared the protesters off the land and demolished the meeting house and other buildings, in a move not unlike that which had occurred at Parihaka 97 years earlier. Two hundred and twenty-two people were arrested.

Joe Hawke and 12 other members of the Ngati Whatua tribe lodged a claim with the Waitangi Tribunal in 1984, and a revised claim was lodged in April 1986. The Tribunal recommended that:

> The public would retain access to the park land currently held as public parks and reserves but ownership of Okahu Park and of the headland parks of Bastion Point would vest in the Ngati Whatua of Orakei Maori Trust Board, while their control and management would vest in a new Reserve Board comprising Ngati Whatua and Auckland City Council representatives.

and that:

> Ngati Whatua, through its Trust Board, would additionally receive 3 hectares for such development as it sees fit, remission of a $200,000 debt, and also $3,000,000 to inaugurate programmes necessary for the tribes rehabilitation. That Ngati Whatua of Orakei Maori Trust Board would be reconstituted as a tribal authority and would have vested in it the Orakei marae, church, and village.

On 1 July 1988 the Government announced that it had agreed to the Tribunal's recommendations.

BIBLIOGRAPHY

Barthorp, Michael (1979). *To Face the Daring Maori: Soldiers' Impressions of the First Maori War. 1845–47.* London, Hodder & Stoughton.

Belich, James (1986). *The New Zealand Wars and the Victorian Interpretation of Racial Conflict.* Auckland, Penguin.

Belich, James (1989). *I Shall Not Die.* Wellington, Allen & Unwin.

Binney, Judith (1995). *Redemption Songs, A Life of Te Kooti Arikirangi Te Turuki.* Auckland, Auckland University Press with Bridget Williams Books.

Cowan, James (1983 edn). *The New Zealand Wars and the Pioneering Period.* Vols 1 and 2. Wellington, Government Printing Office.

Cowan, James (1982). *Tales of the Maori.* Wellington, A. H. & A. W. Reed.

King, Michael (1984 edn). *Maori, A Photographic and Social History.* Auckland, Heinemann Reed.

Lambert, Thomas (1925). *The Story of Old Wairoa and the East Coast.* Dunedin, Coulls, Sommerville, Wilkie.

Laurie, B. Clayton, G. Tonkin-Covell, J. (1990). *Sergeant, Sinner, Saint & Spy. The Taranaki War Diary of Sergeant William Marjouram, R. A.* Auckland, Random Century.

Maning, F. E. (1987 edn). *Old New Zealand, A Tale of the Good Old Times, by a Pakeha Maori.* Auckland, Viking.

MacDonald, Robert (1989). *The Fifth Wind, New Zealand and the Legacy of a Turbulent Past.* London, Bloomsbury.

Pugsley, Christopher. Various articles from *Defence Quarterly* Magazine.

Simpson, Tony (1979). *Te Riri Pakeha: The White Man's Anger.* Martinborough, Alister Taylor.

Sinclair, Keith (1991). *Kinds of Peace.* Auckland, Auckland University Press.

Stowers, Richard (1996). *Forest Rangers: A History of the Forest Rangers During the New Zealand Wars.* Hamilton, Stowers.

Walker, Ranginui (1990). *Ka Whawhai Tonu Matou: Struggle Without End.* Auckland, Penguin.

INDEX

Index